LEMON DE CITRON

The Little Politicians: Adventures in Democracy Land

First published by The Shiba Inu Media Company 2023

First edition

ISBN: 978-1-7389645-4-3

Cover art by Wendy Mitchell
Illustration by Wendy Mitchell

This book was professionally typeset on Reedsy.
Find out more at reedsy.com

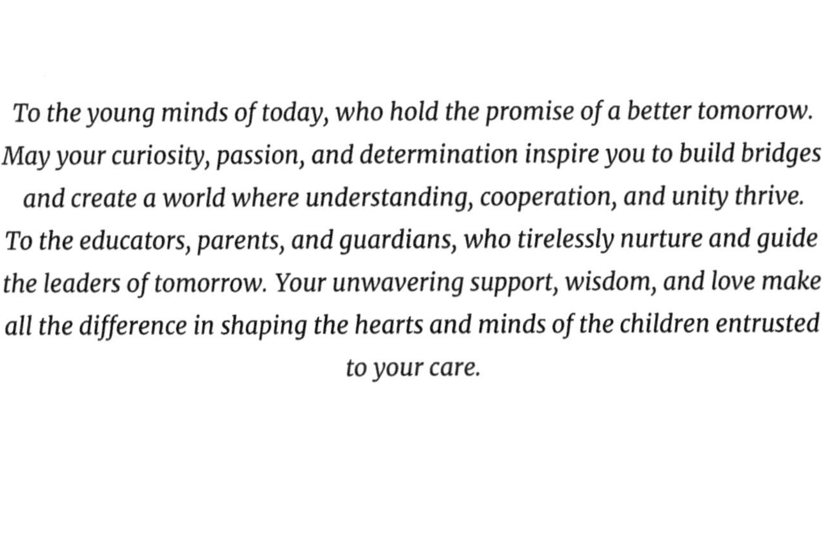

To the young minds of today, who hold the promise of a better tomorrow. May your curiosity, passion, and determination inspire you to build bridges and create a world where understanding, cooperation, and unity thrive. To the educators, parents, and guardians, who tirelessly nurture and guide the leaders of tomorrow. Your unwavering support, wisdom, and love make all the difference in shaping the hearts and minds of the children entrusted to your care.

"In the heart of every child lies the potential to change the world. Through the eyes of the Little Politicians, we discover the power of collaboration, the beauty of diversity, and the boundless spirit of youth. These are the adventures that will shape the leaders of tomorrow, and in their journey, we find hope for a brighter future."

Lemon de Citron

Contents

Preface

In today's fast-paced and ever-changing world, it is more important than ever to instill in our children the values that will guide them as they grow up and become active citizens. The Little Politicians: Adventures in Democracy Land was born from the belief that children are the key to a better future and that by nurturing their natural curiosity and sense of justice, we can empower them to become thoughtful, compassionate, and responsible leaders.

This collection of stories follows the adventures of a group of young friends who share a passion for making a difference in their community. Through their experiences, they learn about the complexities of democracy, the importance of collaboration, and the power of diverse perspectives. Each story is designed to educate and inspire young readers, fostering an appreciation for the democratic process and the crucial role that every individual plays in shaping the world around them.

The Little Politicians encounter a wide range of challenges in their journey, reflecting the many facets of civic engagement and the myriad of issues that communities face. From environmental stewardship and education reform to cultural understanding and conflict resolution, these stories provide valuable lessons on the power of collective action and the potential of every person to make a positive impact.

It is our hope that The Little Politicians: Adventures in Democracy Land will spark meaningful conversations and inspire young readers to explore their own unique passions and interests, recognizing the potential they hold as future leaders and change-makers. In the end, it is the spirit of collaboration, the courage to stand up for what is right, and the willingness to listen and learn from one another that will guide us towards a brighter, more inclusive future.

Join the Little Politicians on their journey through Democracy Land and discover the power of unity, the beauty of diversity, and the boundless potential that lies within each and every one of us.

1

Story 1: The Curious Case of the Vanishing Votes

Part 1: Mysterious Disappearances

In the heart of a lush green valley, surrounded by rolling hills and meandering rivers, lay the charming town of Democracy Land. It was a place where people of all ages, backgrounds, and interests lived together in harmony. The colourful streets bustled with laughter and lively conversations, and the air was filled with the sweet smell of freshly baked pies and blooming flowers.

As the local election approached, excitement rippled through the town like a wave. The citizens of Democracy Land eagerly anticipated this significant event, knowing that their votes could shape the future of their beloved community. Campaign posters adorned every lamppost and shop window, while candidates hosted town hall meetings and shook hands with enthusiastic supporters.

Among the many residents of Democracy Land were four inseparable friends - Lily, a bright and observant girl with a penchant for solving mysteries; Alex, a tech-savvy whiz who could fix any gadget in a blink; Maria, a charismatic and confident leader with an infectious smile; and Ben, a young historian who knew every nook and cranny of the town's rich past. Together, they spent their days exploring the town's hidden gems and embarking on thrilling adventures.

The day before the election, an unsettling rumour spread like wildfire through the town. It seemed that a significant number of votes had mysteriously vanished from the polling station, casting a dark shadow over the upcoming event. Whispered conversations filled the streets as worried citizens speculated about the cause of the missing votes. Fear and suspicion gripped the once-harmonious community.

While hanging out in their secret hideout – an old treehouse overlooking the town – Lily, Alex, Maria, and Ben couldn't help but overhear the anxious murmurs of the adults below. Concerned for the future of Democracy Land, they exchanged determined glances and knew they couldn't stand idly by. They had to do something – and fast. With a resolute nod, the four friends embarked on their most important adventure yet: solving the curious case of the vanishing votes.

Part 2: The Unlikely Detectives

With their hearts filled with determination, the four friends gathered at their treehouse headquarters to devise a plan. They knew that each of them possessed unique talents that, when combined, could be the key to solving the mystery of the vanishing votes.

Lily, her keen eyes always ready to spot the tiniest detail, headed straight to the polling station. She meticulously examined the surroundings, searching for any clues that might have been left behind. Carefully scanning the area, she discovered a set of unusual footprints leading away from the building.

Meanwhile, Alex put on his thinking cap and dove into the world of electronics. As Democracy Land's voting system had recently been upgraded to include electronic components, he suspected that the disappearance might be the result of tampering. With his unmatched technological prowess, he scrutinized the system for any signs of foul play.

Maria, known for her effortless charm and ability to connect with others, set out to interview the townspeople. She approached everyone with kindness and patience, collecting their thoughts, experiences, and any relevant information that might lead to a breakthrough in the investigation.

Ben, the ever-curious historian, buried himself in the archives at the local library. He knew that understanding the town's past could provide valuable context for the current predicament. After hours of poring over old records and newspapers, he uncovered a long-forgotten story of a similar voting issue that had occurred many years ago.

As the sun began to dip below the horizon, the four friends regrouped at the treehouse, their faces alight with the excitement of discovery. They carefully laid out the evidence they had collected and pieced together the puzzle before them. With each clue fitting together like the intricate gears of a clock, the mysterious case of the vanishing votes slowly began to unravel.

Part 3: The Power of Fair Voting

With the clues they had carefully collected, the four friends traced the mysterious footprints to a small, secluded house on the outskirts of Democracy Land. As they cautiously approached the dwelling, they discovered that the missing votes were hidden within, taken by a disgruntled citizen who felt that their voice didn't matter in the grand scheme of things.

With gentle understanding and unwavering conviction, Lily, Alex, Maria, and Ben confronted the troubled individual. They took turns sharing heartfelt stories about the importance of every single vote in a democratic society, emphasizing that each person's voice held power and significance. Moved by the friends' sincerity and the realization that their actions had affected the entire community, the citizen tearfully agreed to help set things right.

Working as a united team, the friends and the remorseful citizen retrieved the missing votes and returned them safely to the polling station, just in time for the election to proceed as planned. The entire town of Democracy Land rejoiced, celebrating the successful event with music, dancing, and delicious treats.

As word spread about the young heroes' extraordinary feat, Lily, Alex, Maria, and Ben were showered with gratitude and admiration. They had not only saved the election but had also restored hope and unity within their community. Through their daring adventure, they had learned a valuable lesson: the power of fair voting and the importance of civic participation in shaping the future of Democracy Land. Together, they vowed to carry this wisdom with them, nurturing the democratic spirit that made their town so special.

2

Story 2: The Mayor's Dilemma

Part 1: The New Mayor

Nestled in a picturesque valley, the town of Democracy Land was a vibrant and thriving community. Its citizens were a diverse and compassionate lot, working together to create an environment where everyone felt welcome and valued. With its quaint cobblestone streets, charming boutiques, and bustling town square, Democracy Land was the epitome of an idyllic small town.

One sunny morning, the townspeople eagerly gathered in the square, anticipation hanging in the air like the sweet scent of freshly baked pastries. It was election day, and a new mayor was about to be chosen to lead Democracy Land. Among the candidates was Emily, a young and passionate woman with a vision to make the town an even better place for all its residents.

Emily had dedicated herself to understanding the needs and aspirations of the community, knocking on doors, attending neighbourhood meetings, and listening intently to the stories and concerns of her fellow citizens. Her campaign was built on a foundation of empathy, collaboration, and the belief that every voice mattered.

As the votes were counted and the results announced, a wave of excitement swept through the crowd. Emily had won the election, becoming the new mayor of Democracy Land. The townspeople erupted in jubilant cheers and applause, their enthusiasm for their new leader contagious. They were eager to see the fresh ideas and energy that Emily would bring to her role, and they believed in her ability to enact positive change.

In the days that followed her inauguration, Emily wasted no time getting to work. She met with town council members, local business owners, and community leaders to discuss pressing issues and brainstorm innovative solutions. It seemed that the future of Democracy Land was bright, and the citizens couldn't have been more proud of their new mayor.

One afternoon, as Emily sat in her office poring over documents and making plans for the town's growth, she received an unexpected piece of news. The town had been granted a substantial sum of money to construct a brand new park, a gift from a generous benefactor who had once called Democracy Land home. The news sent a buzz of excitement throughout the community, as the prospect of a new park presented endless possibilities for both leisure and learning.

Emily knew that the creation of the park was a unique opportunity to further enhance the quality of life for the citizens of Democracy Land. She envisioned a space where children could play and learn, families could gather for picnics, and friends could meet for a leisurely stroll among the greenery. However, she also understood that such a project would require careful planning and consideration to ensure that the needs and desires of the entire community were taken into account.

As the sun dipped below the horizon, casting a warm glow over the town, Emily couldn't help but feel both excited and daunted by the task ahead. She had the power to shape the future of Democracy Land, and with it came the responsibility to make choices that would impact the lives of everyone who called the town their home. Little did she know that her first major decision as mayor would soon present a challenge that would test her leadership skills and reveal the true importance of listening to the people she served.

Part 2: The Difficult Decision

As word of the new park spread throughout Democracy Land, the townspeople eagerly shared their ideas and dreams for the forthcoming project. It wasn't long before two main groups emerged, each with a distinct vision for the park's purpose and design.

On one side were the families, who longed for a safe and inviting space where their children could run, play, and let their imaginations soar. They envisioned a park filled with colourful playground equipment, sports fields, and picnic areas, where the laughter of children would echo through the air and parents could watch with joy as their little ones made new friends.

The second group, comprised of environmentalists and nature lovers, had a different perspective. They saw the park as an opportunity to create a sanctuary for local flora and fauna, preserving and nurturing the natural beauty that made Democracy Land so special. They proposed a nature reserve, complete with walking trails, educational displays, and areas for observing the local wildlife.

Emily found herself torn between the two groups, feeling the weight of her responsibility to make a decision that would impact the entire community. She understood the importance of creating a space for children to play and interact, but also recognized the value of protecting and appreciating the natural environment.

Seeking guidance, Emily consulted her advisors, who presented her with a range of perspectives and considerations. Some argued that the park should cater to the needs of the town's growing population, prioritizing recreational facilities for families. Others highlighted the benefits of nature conservation and the importance of fostering an appreciation for the environment among the citizens of Democracy Land.

Despite the passionate arguments and thoughtful insights, Emily's advisors ultimately left the decision in her hands. As the mayor, it was her responsibility to make the choice that would best serve the community as a whole.

In the quiet solitude of her office, Emily reflected on the passionate voices of the townspeople and the advice of her trusted advisors. She understood that, regardless of her decision, she risked disappointing one group while pleasing the other. The weight of her responsibility settled heavily on her shoulders as she grappled with the challenge of finding a solution that would satisfy the diverse needs and desires of the community she loved.

It was in this moment of contemplation that Emily realized she had overlooked a crucial element in her decision-making process: the opportunity to engage with the people of Democracy Land and truly listen to their thoughts, ideas, and concerns. If she was to make the best possible decision for the town, she needed to ensure that every voice was heard and considered.

With renewed determination, Emily decided to hold a town hall meeting, where all the citizens would have the chance to share their opinions and engage in a meaningful dialogue about the future of the park. By involving the community in the decision-making process, Emily hoped to find a way to balance the competing interests of the town and create a park that would be cherished by all who called Democracy Land home.

Part 3: Listening to the People

With the date for the town hall meeting set, the citizens of Democracy Land eagerly anticipated the opportunity to voice their opinions and contribute to the decision-making process. Emily ensured that everyone in the town was informed and invited, creating an atmosphere of inclusivity and collaboration.

On the evening of the meeting, the town hall buzzed with energy as residents filed in, their faces a mix of hope and determination. Emily stood at the podium, her eyes scanning the room as she prepared to address the crowd. With a deep breath, she welcomed everyone and expressed her gratitude for their attendance and willingness to share their ideas.

As the floor opened for discussion, Emily listened intently to the impassioned arguments and heartfelt stories that emerged from the crowd. She quickly discovered that, despite the seemingly polarized opinions of the two main groups, there were many overlapping interests and shared concerns among the townspeople.

Parents spoke of their desire to in-still a love for nature in their children, while environmentalists acknowledged the importance of having a space for the community to come together and enjoy the outdoors. This common ground sparked a flurry of ideas and suggestions, as people from all walks of life contributed to the conversation.

Inspired by the collective wisdom and creativity of her fellow citizens, Emily began to envision a solution that could harmoniously unite the desires of both groups. A park that combined recreational facilities with a protected natural area, allowing children and families to enjoy outdoor activities while also preserving and celebrating the environment.

As Emily presented her vision to the crowd, a wave of approval and excitement rippled through the room. The townspeople could see the beauty in a park that catered to their diverse needs while fostering a sense of unity and shared purpose. By engaging with the community and genuinely listening to their voices, Emily had found a way to balance the competing interests and create a plan that resonated with the people of Democracy Land.

With the decision made and the town's support behind her, Emily set to work on bringing the park to life. She assembled a team of experts, local volunteers, and enthusiastic citizens who eagerly contributed their time, skills, and ideas to the project. Over time, the park began to take shape, transforming into a beautiful and multifaceted space that reflected the spirit and values of Democracy Land.

As the park's grand opening approached, Emily couldn't help but reflect on the journey that had brought her to this moment. The difficult decision, the town hall meeting, and the invaluable lessons she had learned about the importance of engaging with the community and truly listening to their needs as a leader.

With a warm smile and a heart filled with gratitude, Emily stood before her fellow citizens at the park's inauguration, the sun casting its golden light upon the playground, the walking trails, and the natural habitats that now coexisted in perfect harmony. The joy and pride emanating from the crowd were a testament to the power of collaboration, empathy, and the unwavering belief that every voice, no matter how small, deserved to be heard.

The new park, a living symbol of the unity and shared purpose that defined Democracy Land, would serve as a constant reminder of the importance of listening to the people and the incredible things that could be achieved when a community came together, hand in hand, to create a brighter future for all.

3

Story 3: The Lost City of Compromise

Part 1: The Ancient Map

In the bustling town of Democracy Land, four friends were inseparable. Lily, a deep thinker with a knack for understanding people, was always eager to learn. Alex, a problem solver and technology enthusiast, loved finding answers to the toughest questions. Maria, with her natural leadership and boundless energy, could rally a crowd around any cause. And Ben, a history buff with an insatiable curiosity, had a unique ability to connect the past with the present.

One day, the four friends were exploring the local library, searching for exciting tales and forgotten knowledge hidden within the dusty shelves. As they rummaged through piles of old books and scrolls, Ben came across a tattered tome that caught his attention. The cover was worn, but a faint illustration of an ancient city could still be seen beneath the layers of dust and time.

Excited by their discovery, the friends gathered around as Ben carefully opened the book, revealing a beautifully drawn map tucked within its pages. The map depicted a winding path through a mysterious forest, leading to the fabled Lost City of Compromise. According to the legend, this city was a place where people had mastered the art of compromise, creating a society that thrived on balance and harmony.

Intrigued by the tale, Lily, Alex, Maria, and Ben felt a shared desire to uncover the secrets of the Lost City of Compromise. They believed that learning the art of compromise would help them better navigate the complexities of their own lives and contribute positively to their beloved town of Democracy Land.

With a sense of adventure in their hearts, the friends decided to embark on a journey to find the Lost City of Compromise. They prepared carefully, gathering supplies, planning their route, and studying the ancient map to ensure they could navigate the treacherous terrain that lay ahead. As they made their final preparations, the friends felt a mixture of excitement and nervous anticipation. They knew that their adventure would test their resilience, their resourcefulness, and, above all, their ability to work together as a team.

As the day of departure arrived, Lily, Alex, Maria, and Ben stood at the edge of the mysterious Debate Forest, which the map indicated as the first stage of their journey. They gazed into the dense foliage, where trees of all shapes and sizes seemed to stretch endlessly into the distance. The forest appeared to be alive with whispers and rustling leaves, as if countless voices were engaged in a never-ending conversation.

With a deep breath and a determined gaze, the friends stepped into the forest, leaving the familiar sights and sounds of Democracy Land behind. They knew that the journey ahead would be filled with challenges, as they navigated the labyrinth of opinions and ideas that existed within Debate Forest. But they were driven by a shared passion to uncover the secrets of the Lost City of Compromise, and the valuable lessons it held about the art of finding balance amid disagreement.

United by their common goal, Lily, Alex, Maria, and Ben ventured deeper into Debate Forest, their hearts full of hope and determination. They were eager to learn the secrets of the Lost City of Compromise and, in doing so, strengthen the bonds of friendship that tied them together. And with each step they took, the friends knew that they were embarking on an adventure that would change their lives and their understanding of the world around them forever.

Part 2: The Journey Through Debate Forest

As the friends ventured deeper into Debate Forest, they began to discover the unique nature of their surroundings. The trees, they realized, were not ordinary trees; they represented different opinions and viewpoints, their branches and leaves whispering with the voices of countless arguments and debates.

The creatures of the forest, too, were unlike any they had encountered before. Each animal embodied a particular perspective, and as the friends moved through the forest, they found themselves engaging with these creatures in discussions about various topics and dilemmas. From the wise old owl, who sought balance in every situation, to the spirited squirrel, who fervently defended its beliefs, the friends were exposed to an incredible array of ideas and opinions.

As they continued on their journey, Lily, Alex, Maria, and Ben faced numerous challenges. The path through Debate Forest was often obscured by tangled vines and thorny bushes, representing the complexities and conflicts that arose from the clashing opinions. They quickly realized that in order to navigate the forest successfully, they would need to listen, understand, and appreciate the perspectives of others.

One day, the friends came across a wide river that seemed impossible to cross. The river, they learned, represented the divide between two opposing viewpoints. On one side, the creatures argued passionately for the importance of progress and innovation, while on the other, the animals defended the value of tradition and stability.

Feeling disheartened, the friends huddled together, trying to figure out a way to bridge the gap between the two sides. It was then that Lily had an idea. She suggested that they listen carefully to the concerns and aspirations of both groups and use their newfound understanding to find a solution that respected and incorporated the perspectives of all.

With renewed determination, the friends spent the next several days engaging in conversations with the creatures on both sides of the river. They listened intently, seeking to understand the fears, hopes, and dreams that fuelled the impassioned arguments. Through these conversations, the friends began to see the value in empathy and open-mindedness, as they discovered that each perspective held its own wisdom and merit.

Armed with this newfound understanding, the friends came up with a plan. They gathered materials from the forest and built a bridge that spanned the river, allowing the creatures from both sides to come together and share their ideas. In doing so, they facilitated a dialogue that allowed the animals to see the strengths and validity of each other's perspectives, ultimately leading to a harmonious blend of progress and tradition.

As they crossed the bridge and continued their journey through Debate Forest, Lily, Alex, Maria, and Ben felt a profound sense of accomplishment. They had successfully navigated the complexities of conflicting viewpoints and found a path forward amid disagreement. They now understood that the art of compromise was rooted in empathy, open-mindedness, and the ability to appreciate the perspectives of others.

With this valuable lesson ingrained in their hearts, the friends pressed on, eager to reach the Lost City of Compromise and uncover the secrets that awaited them. As they moved through the forest, the friends knew that they had grown stronger, not just as individuals, but as a team united by their shared commitment to understanding and cooperation. And as the Lost City of Compromise drew closer with each step, they couldn't help but feel excited about the challenges and discoveries that still lay ahead.

Part 3: Finding Balance

After many days of journeying through Debate Forest, the friends finally arrived at the Lost City of Compromise. As they entered the city gates, they were struck by its beauty and harmony. The architecture was a perfect blend of different styles, seamlessly merging the old with the new. The city's gardens were a testament to balance and cooperation, with plants and flowers from diverse ecosystems coexisting in lush harmony.

As they explored the city, Lily, Alex, Maria, and Ben couldn't help but notice the peaceful atmosphere that seemed to permeate every corner of the Lost City. The people they encountered were kind and respectful, engaging in thoughtful conversations that demonstrated a genuine appreciation for differing opinions.

It wasn't long before the friends were introduced to the wise elder of the city. The elder, a kind and gentle figure with a wealth of experience, welcomed the friends warmly and commended them for their bravery in undertaking the journey to the Lost City of Compromise.

Eager to learn the secret to mastering the art of compromise, the friends asked the elder for guidance. The elder smiled and began to share the wisdom that had been passed down through generations in the Lost City.

"The secret to compromise," the elder explained, "lies in the ability to listen, understand, and find common ground. When we truly listen to others, we open ourselves up to new ideas and perspectives, allowing us to see the world through their eyes."

The elder continued, "True compromise is not about giving up one's beliefs or surrendering one's values. Rather, it is about finding a way to create solutions that benefit everyone involved. By seeking to understand the needs and desires of others, we can work together to forge a path forward that honours the perspectives of all."

As they absorbed the elder's words, the friends realized that their journey through Debate Forest had been the perfect training ground for learning the art of compromise. They had navigated conflicting viewpoints, found a path forward amid disagreement, and discovered the importance of empathy and open-mindedness in resolving conflicts.

With their newfound wisdom, Lily, Alex, Maria, and Ben knew that it was time to return to Democracy Land. They thanked the elder and the people of the Lost City for their guidance and hospitality before embarking on the journey home, eager to share their knowledge with their fellow citizens.

Upon their return to Democracy Land, the friends put their newfound understanding of compromise into practice. They worked together to promote harmony and cooperation within their community, helping to resolve disputes and foster greater understanding between people with differing opinions.

As they applied the lessons they had learned from the Lost City of Compromise, the friends discovered that their adventure had changed not only their own lives but also the lives of those around them. By championing the art of compromise, they had created an environment in which every voice could be heard, and every perspective valued.

In the end, Lily, Alex, Maria, and Ben realized that the true power of compromise lay in its ability to bring people together, bridging divides and fostering a sense of unity that allowed their community to thrive. And as they looked back on their incredible journey, the friends knew that they had uncovered a treasure far more valuable than any ancient city: the power of understanding, balance, and harmony in a world of diverse opinions.

4

Story 4: The Great Election Race

Part 1: The Candidates

In the bustling town of Democracy Land, excitement filled the air as the citizens prepared for an important election that would determine their next leader. Colourful banners adorned the streets, and lively conversations echoed in every corner of the town square. The people of Democracy Land understood the significance of this election and were eager to participate in the democratic process.

Two main candidates were vying for the coveted position: Sarah, a seasoned politician with years of experience under her belt, and James, a newcomer to the political scene with a passion for preserving traditions and stability. Both candidates held strong convictions and presented distinct visions for the future of Democracy Land.

Sarah, known for her progressive ideas and innovative mindset, campaigned on a platform centred around modernizing the town's infrastructure and embracing new technologies. Her rallies were energetic, and her supporters often donned bright colours and carried signs with slogans like "Progress for a Better Tomorrow" and "Innovation is Our Future." Sarah's speeches were articulate and well-researched, leaving her audience inspired and hopeful for the future of Democracy Land.

On the other hand, James, a staunch advocate for preserving the town's traditions and values, focused on maintaining stability in the community. His campaign events had a nostalgic atmosphere, with supporters dressed in historical attire, and signs that read "Preserve Our Heritage" and "Stability for a Stronger Community." James's speeches emphasized the importance of honouring the past, learning from the town's history, and ensuring that the core values of Democracy Land remained intact.

As the election campaign progressed, the citizens of Democracy Land grew increasingly engaged in the process. They attended rallies, asked questions, and discussed the candidates' proposals with friends and neighbours. Conversations at the local cafe buzzed with excitement, as people debated the merits of progress versus tradition, and innovation versus stability.

The town's community centre became a hub of activity, hosting regular meetings where citizens could gather to share their thoughts and opinions on the election. People from all walks of life attended these meetings, highlighting the diversity of Democracy Land's citizenry and the wide range of perspectives they brought to the table. The spirit of democracy was alive and well, as the people of Democracy Land eagerly participated in shaping the future of their community.

As the election drew nearer, the anticipation reached a fever pitch. The citizens of Democracy Land knew that the outcome of this election would have a lasting impact on their town, and they were committed to making an informed decision. It was in this atmosphere of excitement and engagement that Sarah and James prepared to face off in a crucial event that would allow the citizens to compare their visions directly: the big debate.

Part 2: The Big Debate

The town of Democracy Land buzzed with anticipation as the date for the big debate approached. Both Sarah and James were set to present their ideas and plans, providing the citizens an opportunity to compare their visions for the community directly. The local newspaper, "The Democracy Land Daily," announced the debate on the front page, accompanied by an illustration of the two candidates standing behind podiums, ready for a lively discussion.

In the days leading up to the debate, Sarah and James dedicated themselves to refining their arguments and perfecting their talking points. They consulted with advisors, practiced their speeches, and reviewed the concerns of the citizens to ensure they were well-prepared to address the most pressing issues facing Democracy Land. Meanwhile, the citizens eagerly awaited the event, discussing their expectations and predictions with friends, family, and neighbours.

On the day of the debate, the town's community centre was packed to the brim, with every seat filled and additional viewers watching the live broadcast on screens set up outside. The atmosphere was electric as the moderator took the stage, welcoming the audience and outlining the rules of the debate.

The debate kicked off with opening statements from both candidates. Sarah began by reiterating her commitment to progress and innovation, emphasizing the importance of embracing change to propel Democracy Land into a brighter future. James followed, reminding the audience of the rich history of the town and the value of preserving its traditions and stability.

As the debate progressed, the candidates engaged in a lively back-and-forth, showcasing their contrasting views and their ability to articulate their positions clearly. Sarah outlined her plans to invest in renewable energy and modernize the town's public transportation system, while James argued for the preservation of historical landmarks and maintaining the town's unique character.

The moderator posed questions from the citizens, ranging from topics such as education, healthcare, and community safety. The candidates were challenged to address these issues, and the audience listened intently to their responses. Sarah and James demonstrated their knowledge and passion for their respective platforms, yet also showed respect and civility towards each other, setting an example of constructive dialogue.

Throughout the debate, the citizens of Democracy Land gained a deeper understanding of the candidates' proposals, allowing them to make a more informed decision on Election Day. They appreciated the opportunity to witness the candidates engaging in a spirited discussion, as it helped them to better grasp the nuances of each candidate's ideas and consider the implications of their choices.

By the end of the debate, the citizens of Democracy Land felt more confident in their understanding of the candidates and their platforms. They knew that their decision would shape the future of their town, and they were grateful for the democratic process that allowed them to have a say in the matter. As the citizens left the community centre and dispersed into the night, they knew that the big debate had played a pivotal role in their journey towards making the people's choice.

Part 3: The People's Choice

Election Day arrived in Democracy Land, and the sun rose on a town filled with anticipation and determination. The citizens, eager to participate in the democratic process and have their voices heard, flocked to the polls early in the morning. Lines formed outside the voting booths, with people chatting animatedly about their experiences during the campaign season and sharing their hopes for the future of their town.

Parents brought their children along, teaching them the significance of exercising their right to vote and the importance of active civic engagement. The atmosphere was one of community and shared purpose, as the citizens of Democracy Land united to cast their ballots and help shape the future of their beloved town.

As the day wore on, the last of the voters made their way to the polls, and the sense of anticipation grew palpable. The town square was abuzz with activity as people gathered to await the election results. As the evening sky darkened, the moment finally arrived: the results were announced, and a winner emerged after a closely contested race.

Sarah, the candidate advocating for progress and innovation, had won the election by a narrow margin. Her supporters erupted in cheers and applause, celebrating the victory and the promise of a bright future for Democracy Land. Sarah took to the stage to address her supporters, expressing her gratitude and pledging to work tirelessly to fulfill her campaign promises and improve the lives of the citizens.

James, the losing candidate, graciously accepted the outcome of the election. He congratulated Sarah on her victory and urged his supporters to come together and support the new leader for the betterment of the town. James's speech highlighted the importance of unity and grace in accepting the election results, acknowledging that Democracy Land would only thrive if its citizens worked together, regardless of their differing views.

The citizens of Democracy Land, regardless of which candidate they had supported, celebrated their participation in the democratic process. They had learned the value of informed decision-making, active civic engagement, and the importance of dialogue and debate in shaping the future of their community. As the night wore on and the celebrations continued, the people of Democracy Land took pride in the knowledge that their collective efforts had contributed to the town's vibrant democracy.

In the days that followed, the town slowly returned to its usual rhythms, but the lessons of the election campaign and the big debate remained fresh in the citizens' minds. They knew that the democratic process was an ongoing journey, one that required continuous engagement, discussion, and compromise to ensure the well-being of their community.

As Sarah began her term as the leader of Democracy Land, she carried with her the hopes and aspirations of the people who had entrusted her with their future. The citizens, too, recognized their responsibility to remain involved and hold their leaders accountable, ensuring that the democratic spirit that had guided them through the election would continue to flourish in their town for years to come.

5

Story 5: The Magical Voting Booth

Part 1: The Mysterious Box

One sunny afternoon in Democracy Land, four friends – Lily, Alex, Maria, and Ben – were exploring the old storage room in the town hall. The room was filled with fascinating relics of the town's past, from dusty books and scrolls to peculiar gadgets that seemed to have been forgotten by time. The friends loved nothing more than to embark on new adventures and learn about the history of their beloved town.

As they carefully maneuvered their way through the dimly lit room, Alex accidentally stumbled upon a dusty tarp covering a mysterious, antique box. "Hey, look at this!" he exclaimed, attracting the attention of his friends. Together, they pulled back the tarp, revealing a beautifully crafted, old-fashioned voting booth. Intricate engravings adorned the wooden surface, and the booth seemed to radiate an aura of mystery and magic.

Their curiosity piqued, the friends inspected the booth, marvelling at the detailed craftsmanship. Inside the booth, Maria discovered a faded, yellowed note. She carefully unfolded it and read the delicate handwriting aloud: "To whomever finds this magical voting booth, know that it has the power to transport its users through time to different eras of democracy. Use it wisely and learn from the past to shape a better future."

The friends exchanged glances, excitement and disbelief in their eyes. Time travel was the stuff of dreams and legends, but the note's message stirred something within them. They couldn't help but wonder if the booth could truly take them on such an incredible journey.

After a moment of contemplation, Lily spoke up. "What if we gave it a try? It might just be a story, but imagine the adventures we could have and the lessons we could learn about democracy!" Her friends nodded in agreement, their hearts racing with anticipation.

One by one, the friends stepped into the magical voting booth, their fingers hovering over the antique levers. As they prepared to cast their votes, they couldn't help but feel the weight of history and the power of democracy at their fingertips. With a mixture of excitement and trepidation, they each cast their vote, ready to embark on a time-traveling adventure unlike any they had ever experienced before.

Part 2: The Time-Traveling Vote

As the friends took turns stepping into the magical voting booth, the room seemed to buzz with anticipation. Each vote cast sent them hurtling through time and space, landing them in different historical periods where they would bear witness to pivotal moments in the history of democracy.

Lily found herself transported to the women's suffrage movement, surrounded by passionate women clad in white and purple, marching through the streets and demanding the right to vote. She watched in awe as they faced ridicule and resistance, their unyielding determination to secure a voice for women resonating deeply within her. Lily marvelled at their courage and resilience, realizing that she owed her own right to vote to these trailblazing women.

Meanwhile, Alex was thrust into the heart of the Civil Rights Movement, observing brave men and women fighting for equal voting rights for all citizens, regardless of race. He witnessed the tireless efforts of activists like Martin Luther King Jr., who inspired millions with his vision of a just and equal society. As he stood among the marchers, Alex felt humbled by their sacrifices and grateful for the progress they made in ensuring that every voice counted in the democratic process.

Maria's journey took her to a distant land in the throes of revolution, where people from all walks of life were fighting for the establishment of a democratic government. She watched as they rose up against tyranny and oppression, their shared desire for freedom and self-determination fuelling their struggle. Maria was struck by the resilience and determination of the people she encountered, who were willing to risk everything for the chance to build a better future.

Ben arrived in the early days of Democracy Land, where he learned about the founding principles of the town and the efforts made to create a fair and just society. He observed the first town meetings and saw the birth of the democratic processes that shaped his beloved community. As he delved into the town's history, Ben gained a deeper understanding of the importance of civic participation and the power of the collective voice.

After their individual adventures, the friends reunited in the present day, their minds and hearts overflowing with the stories and lessons they had gleaned from their journeys. As they shared their experiences, they marvelled at the strength and determination of the people they had encountered, each of whom had played a vital role in shaping the history of democracy.

Together, they realized that they had been granted a priceless gift: a newfound appreciation for the democratic process and a deeper understanding of the power of every voice in shaping the world around them.

Part 3: The Importance of Every Voice

As the friends returned to the present day, they couldn't shake the feeling of awe and inspiration that their time-traveling adventures had ignited within them. They had witnessed firsthand the sacrifices made by those who fought for democracy, and the pivotal moments in history that had shaped their world.

The experience left them with a deep appreciation for the importance of every citizen's voice and the impact that voting could have on shaping the future. They understood now, more than ever, that democracy was a precious gift, one that had been hard-earned by the determination and resilience of countless individuals throughout history.

Determined to make a difference, Lily, Alex, Maria, and Ben became more engaged in their community. They attended town meetings, joined local organizations, and volunteered their time to support causes they believed in. They encouraged their friends and neighbours to participate in the democratic process, stressing the value of voting and the power that each voice held in influencing the direction of their community.

As the next local election approached, the friends could hardly contain their excitement. They had spent weeks educating themselves about the candidates and their platforms, eager to make an informed decision and contribute to the future of Democracy Land.

On Election Day, they stood together in line at the polling station, their hearts swelling with pride as they waited for their turn to cast their votes. They couldn't help but reflect on their journey and the lessons they had learned about the power of every voice in a democratic society.

As they exited the voting booth one by one, they knew that they had done more than simply cast a ballot; they had become a part of the rich tapestry of history, joining the ranks of those who had come before them in the fight for democracy.

The story concludes with the friends gathered together, watching the election results roll in. Regardless of the outcome, they knew that they had made a difference, not just by casting their votes but by embracing their roles as active citizens in their community.

Their time-traveling adventure had taught them a valuable lesson: that the power of every voice, when united in pursuit of a better future, could change the course of history. And as they looked around at their fellow citizens, they couldn't help but feel a sense of gratitude for the opportunity to be a part of the ever-evolving story of democracy.

6

Story 6: The Balanced Budget Adventure

Part 1: The Money Mystery

In the bustling town of Democracy Land, people went about their daily lives, enjoying the services and amenities that the town provided. However, a cloud of worry hung over the town leaders as they grappled with a financial crisis. The town's budget was facing a significant deficit, and they were struggling to find a solution that would not harm essential services for the townspeople.

One sunny afternoon, the four friends, Lily, Alex, Maria, and Ben, were sitting on a bench in the town square, sharing stories and laughs. Their carefree chatter was interrupted when they overheard a conversation between two town leaders, discussing the budget crisis and the difficult decisions that lay ahead.

Lily's eyes widened as she listened intently. "Guys, our town is in trouble. We can't just stand by and watch things fall apart. We need to do something!"

Alex nodded in agreement, his curiosity piqued by the challenge. Maria, never one to shy away from taking action, chimed in, "Let's go to the town hall and see if we can help. We might not be experts, but we can at least try to understand the situation."

With determination in their eyes, the friends headed to the town hall, where they were greeted by a friendly receptionist. "Excuse me," Maria began, "we overheard that there's a budget crisis happening in Democracy Land, and we'd like to help. Could we have access to the budget documents?"

The receptionist hesitated for a moment, unsure if the young friends could genuinely offer any assistance. But she admired their enthusiasm and decided to grant their request. "I'll let the town leaders know you're here. Wait here while I get the documents for you."

As the friends waited, they discussed their plan of action. "We need to find out where the money is going and figure out how to balance the budget without causing too much disruption to the town," Ben said.

Lily, ever the analytical thinker, added, "We'll have to review the budget thoroughly and identify any areas where we can make adjustments."

Finally, the receptionist returned with a large binder filled with pages upon pages of numbers, charts, and graphs. She placed it on a table in the centre of the room, and the friends gathered around, eager to dive into the complex world of the town's finances. Little did they know, they were about to embark on an adventure that would teach them the importance of making wise choices and finding balance in resource allocation.

Part 2: Saving the Town's Treasure

The friends decided to tackle the budget problem by dividing tasks according to their strengths. Lily, with her exceptional analytical skills, took on the responsibility of examining the numbers, looking for patterns and trends. Alex, a natural researcher, delved into the town's various income sources, trying to identify any untapped potential. Maria, focused and detail-oriented, studied the expenses, scrutinizing each line item to determine its necessity. And Ben, a resourceful problem-solver, explored possible cost-saving measures that could be implemented without sacrificing the quality of essential services.

As they worked, the friends uncovered several areas of the budget that could be adjusted to create a better balance between income and expenses. They found that some expenses could be reduced by consolidating services, while others could be temporarily postponed without causing long-term harm. Additionally, they discovered opportunities for increasing revenue by optimizing existing income sources, such as adjusting fees for certain services or improving the efficiency of the town's operations.

Armed with their findings, the friends approached the town leaders, eager to present their ideas. The leaders, initially skeptical that a group of young citizens could provide a viable solution, agreed to listen to their proposal.

Lily began the presentation, confidently explaining their analysis of the budget and the patterns they had identified. Alex then detailed the untapped potential they had discovered in the town's income sources, presenting a clear plan for optimizing revenue generation. Maria followed, outlining the adjustments they proposed for the town's expenses, demonstrating how these changes could maintain essential services while reducing the budget deficit. Finally, Ben presented their cost-saving measures, emphasizing the importance of finding a balance between fiscal responsibility and the welfare of the townspeople.

As the friends concluded their presentation, the town leaders exchanged glances, surprised by the depth of understanding and thoroughness the young citizens had demonstrated. One leader spoke up, "We must admit, your proposal is quite impressive. It's clear that you've put a lot of thought and effort into finding a solution for our town's financial crisis."

Another leader chimed in, "We'll need to carefully review your ideas and discuss them among ourselves, but we appreciate your dedication to helping our community. Thank you for your hard work."

The friends left the town hall, feeling a sense of accomplishment and pride in their efforts to save Democracy Land's treasure: the well-being and prosperity of its citizens. And while the town leaders deliberated, the friends knew that their journey had already taught them valuable lessons about working together, being resourceful, and the importance of making wise choices for the greater good.

Part 3: Making Wise Choices

As the town leaders deliberated over the friends' budget proposal, the citizens of Democracy Land waited anxiously for their decision. The financial crisis had taken a toll on the town, and everyone hoped for a resolution that would benefit the entire community.

After several days of careful review, the town leaders called a public meeting to announce their decision. They had thoroughly examined the friends' plan, considering the balance of cutting non-essential expenses, increasing income through innovative measures, and prioritizing essential services. The leaders had concluded that the friends' proposal was indeed a viable solution to the financial crisis.

Standing in front of the gathered citizens, the town's mayor addressed the crowd. "We have carefully reviewed the budget plan presented to us by Lily, Alex, Maria, and Ben. We believe that their proposal offers a fair and balanced approach to resolving our financial crisis. We have decided to implement their suggestions, making the necessary adjustments to our budget to ensure the stability and prosperity of Democracy Land."

A wave of relief and joy swept through the crowd as the citizens celebrated the positive outcome. The friends beamed with pride, knowing that their hard work and dedication had made a difference for their community.

Over the following months, the town leaders put the friends' budget plan into action. Non-essential expenses were reduced, and innovative measures were implemented to increase income. Throughout the process, essential services were carefully prioritized to ensure that the needs of the townspeople were met.

As the changes took effect, Democracy Land gradually overcame the financial crisis. The town's newfound stability was a testament to the power of wise choices and the importance of finding balance when allocating resources for the greater good.

The citizens of Democracy Land celebrated their victory over the crisis with a grand festival, and the four friends were hailed as heroes. The friends had not only saved their town from financial ruin but had also learned invaluable lessons about the importance of making wise choices, working together, and finding balance in their lives and their community.

As the festivities carried on into the night, Lily, Alex, Maria, and Ben took a moment to reflect on their journey. They realized that the key to their success had been their ability to combine their unique talents and perspectives to create a solution that benefited everyone.

Standing together, the friends knew that they had not only made a difference in Democracy Land, but had also grown as individuals, gaining wisdom and understanding that would serve them well in their future endeavours. And as they looked out over the town they had helped to save, they felt an overwhelming sense of pride, knowing that they had played a crucial role in preserving the well-being of their community.

7

Story 7: The Constitution Treasure Hunt

Part 1: The Hidden Clues

In the quaint town of Democracy Land, four friends - Lily, Alex, Maria, and Ben - shared a passion for history and the story of their beloved town. Each friend brought unique skills and interests to the table, making them an inseparable group in their quest for knowledge.

One day, while attending a history class about Democracy Land's Constitution, the friends were captivated by the story of a lost founding document that predated the current Constitution. This document, their professor explained, was believed to contain principles that formed the basis of their society. Intrigued by the possibility of finding this mysterious and historically significant document, the friends decided to embark on a treasure hunt.

After class, they gathered at their favourite coffee shop, excitedly discussing the legend of the lost founding document. They brainstormed where they might find the first clue to the treasure and ultimately agreed that the local library, known for its extensive collection of historical records, was their best bet.

The following day, the friends met at the library and began their search. They combed through shelves of dusty books, scoured old newspapers, and examined ancient artifacts. Lily, with her sharp eye for detail, noticed a peculiar mark on the spine of a seemingly unremarkable book. The mark, which resembled the emblem of Democracy Land, piqued their interest.

Upon opening the book, they found a set of hidden clues - riddles and cryptic messages that seemed to be connected to the lost founding document. The friends' excitement was palpable as they realized that the mysterious treasure they were seeking might be within their reach.

The library began to close, forcing the friends to leave for the day. They made a pact to meet at Lily's house the next day to work on deciphering the hidden clues. With a renewed sense of purpose and determination, they believed that they were on the verge of a monumental discovery that could reshape their understanding of Democracy Land's history.

That night, the friends couldn't help but dream of the treasure hunt that lay ahead. They knew that uncovering the lost founding document would be no easy feat, but they were more than ready to face the challenge together. For each of them, it was not just about the thrill of the hunt, but also about uncovering the roots of their beloved town and learning more about the principles that had shaped their society. Little did they know that their adventure was about to take them on a journey through history, testing their knowledge, their courage, and their friendship.

Part 2: The Journey Through Rights and Responsibilities

The following day, the friends gathered at Lily's house, eager to decipher the hidden clues they had discovered in the library. They spent hours poring over the riddles and cryptic messages, attempting to make sense of them. Finally, they uncovered a pattern: each clue led to a significant historical event or location in Democracy Land.

With a renewed sense of excitement, the friends set out on their journey, following the trail of clues that would guide them through the rights and responsibilities of citizens and the core principles of their society. Their adventure would take them to places they had never seen before, and along the way, they would learn valuable lessons about their community and themselves.

Their first stop was the site of the famous Democracy Land Convention, where leaders from across the town had gathered long ago to debate and draft the current Constitution. Here, the friends learned about the importance of free speech and the right to assemble. They discussed the value of expressing one's opinions and engaging in constructive debates. This experience taught them the significance of these rights and how they contribute to a strong and fair society.

Next, they visited the historical courthouse, where they witnessed a trial in progress. They observed the right to a fair trial and the principles of due process, understanding the importance of holding all citizens accountable under the law. The friends were struck by the wisdom and fairness of the legal system, recognizing that the rule of law was a cornerstone of their democratic society.

As the friends continued their journey, they faced various challenges that tested their knowledge of democracy and their ability to work together as a team. At each location, they encountered puzzles and riddles that required them to recall the democratic principles they had learned and apply them in creative ways. These challenges brought them closer together, strengthening their bond and deepening their appreciation for the democratic values that shaped their community.

One of the most impactful stops on their journey was the Democracy Land Memorial, a monument dedicated to the town's citizens who had fought and sacrificed for their democratic ideals. The friends were moved by the stories of bravery and perseverance, understanding the responsibility each citizen had in upholding and protecting their democracy.

As they neared the end of their journey, the friends arrived at the Hall of Records, a vast archive containing the town's most important documents and historical artifacts. They were in awe of the knowledge and wisdom contained within its walls, realizing that the democratic principles they had learned were the result of generations of citizens working together to create a fair and just society.

With the final clue in hand, the friends felt closer than ever to discovering the lost founding document. They knew that their journey through the rights and responsibilities of citizens had prepared them for this moment. As they stood at the threshold of their ultimate destination, they were filled with a deep sense of gratitude for the democratic principles and values that had guided their journey and shaped their beloved community.

Part 3: The Discovery of the Founding Document

Following the last clue, the friends found themselves standing in front of a hidden chamber within the Hall of Records. They exchanged nervous glances, each one filled with excitement and anticipation. With a deep breath, they pushed open the chamber door, revealing a dimly lit room filled with ancient artifacts and scrolls.

As they entered the chamber, they noticed a pedestal in the centre of the room, illuminated by a beam of light from a hidden window above. Upon the pedestal lay the object of their quest: the long-lost founding document of Democracy Land. The friends exchanged looks of awe and wonder as they carefully approached the historic treasure.

They carefully lifted the document from its resting place and examined its contents. It was beautifully penned in elegant calligraphy, and the parchment bore the weight of history. As they read the words, they discovered that the document contained the original principles upon which Democracy Land was built, many of which were still relevant and cherished today.

Overwhelmed with a sense of accomplishment and responsibility, the friends agreed to bring the founding document to the town leaders, who would understand its significance and ensure its preservation. They carefully wrapped the document and made their way to the town hall, their hearts swelling with pride and gratitude for the lessons they had learned on their journey.

At the town hall, they presented their discovery to the mayor and other town leaders. The room fell silent as the leaders examined the document, their faces reflecting a mixture of awe and reverence. Recognizing the document's historic importance and its relevance to the town's core values, the mayor decided to display it in a prominent location as a reminder of Democracy Land's roots and the principles that continued to guide the community.

A grand ceremony was held to unveil the founding document, and the entire town gathered to celebrate the friends' remarkable discovery. As the friends stood before their fellow citizens, they recounted their adventure and the lessons they had learned about the importance of rights, responsibilities, and the core principles of democracy.

The people of Democracy Land were moved by the friends' story and expressed their gratitude for their dedication and perseverance. The rediscovery of the founding document served as a powerful reminder of the town's heritage and the enduring significance of its democratic principles.

As the ceremony concluded, the friends stood together, their eyes shining with pride and accomplishment. They knew that their adventure had not only helped them uncover a priceless piece of history but had also deepened their understanding of the principles that made their town a shining example of democracy.

With the founding document now prominently displayed in Democracy Land, the friends knew that future generations would be inspired by the same principles and values that had guided their journey. They had played a part in preserving their town's rich history and ensuring that the lessons of the past would continue to shape the future of their beloved community.

8

Story 8: The Peaceful Protest Parade

Part 1: The Unfair Rule

In the vibrant town of Democracy Land, fairness and freedom were the bedrock principles that shaped the lives of its citizens. The people took pride in their open and inclusive community, where each individual had an equal opportunity to thrive and contribute to the greater good. Nestled in the heart of this idyllic town, the four friends – Lily, Alex, Maria, and Ben – had grown up surrounded by democratic values that they held dear.

One sunny afternoon, an unexpected announcement from the local government sent ripples of unease through the community. The town leaders had introduced a new rule that threatened the very essence of democracy in Democracy Land. This rule imposed heavy restrictions on the freedom of speech, limiting the citizens' ability to voice their opinions on critical issues.

Distressed by the unjust nature of this rule, Lily, Alex, Maria, and Ben gathered in their favourite spot at the local park to discuss the situation. They knew they couldn't stand idly by while the core principles of their town were being eroded. As the sun dipped below the horizon, they made a unanimous decision: they would take a stand against the rule by organizing a peaceful protest parade.

The friends knew that organizing such an event would require careful planning and dedication. They divided the tasks among themselves, with Lily taking charge of creating eye-catching signs that conveyed their message, Alex using his knack for communication to spread the word through social media and face-to-face interactions, Maria tapping into her organizational skills to coordinate the logistics of the parade, and Ben liaising with local authorities to ensure the protest remained peaceful and law-abiding.

As the days passed, word of the protest spread like wildfire. The citizens of Democracy Land, who cherished their democratic rights, were eager to stand together against the oppressive rule. The impending parade became a symbol of hope and unity for the townspeople, a testament to their collective strength in the face of adversity.

With each new volunteer that joined their cause, the friends felt a growing sense of responsibility to ensure that the protest remained a peaceful and respectful demonstration of the town's values. They held meetings to discuss the importance of nonviolence and cooperation, emphasizing that the success of their movement hinged on their ability to express their dissent without resorting to aggression or hostility. The message resonated with the citizens, who were determined to show the world that Democracy Land could challenge injustice through the power of unity, empathy, and understanding.

Part 2: The Power of Unity

The day of the protest parade finally arrived, and the air was filled with a palpable sense of anticipation. The citizens of Democracy Land gathered in the town square, a sea of determined faces and colourful signs proclaiming their opposition to the unjust rule. Lily, Alex, Maria, and Ben stood at the forefront, proud of what they had accomplished and eager to lead their community in a display of unity and solidarity.

As the parade began to wind its way through the streets of Democracy Land, more and more people joined the ranks of the protestors. Neighbours called out words of encouragement from their windows, shopkeepers closed their doors to march alongside the throngs of people, and even passersby couldn't help but be drawn to the spirit of camaraderie that permeated the air. The parade gained momentum, its message of unity and opposition to the unjust rule resonating with everyone who bore witness to the peaceful procession.

The power of unity was on full display as the townspeople marched shoulder to shoulder, a living testament to the strength of their collective voice. Each individual brought their unique perspective to the cause, but together, they represented the unwavering commitment of Democracy Land to uphold the principles of fairness and freedom that defined their community.

Despite the shared frustration and anger that had brought the citizens together, the protest parade remained a peaceful and respectful demonstration. The friends had made it clear from the very beginning that their message would be most effective if it was delivered with dignity and restraint. As the parade moved through the town, the protestors engaged in thoughtful discussions, sang songs of hope, and chanted slogans that captured the essence of their cause. There was no hint of violence or aggression, only an unwavering commitment to nonviolent resistance and the pursuit of justice.

Throughout the parade, Lily, Alex, Maria, and Ben marvelled at the sight of their community united in opposition to the unjust rule. They had sparked a movement that brought the citizens of Democracy Land together in a powerful show of unity and resolve. As the parade came to a close, the friends knew that they had played a pivotal role in demonstrating the strength of their community's convictions and the power of peaceful protest to effect change.

As the sun set on the peaceful protest parade, the citizens of Democracy Land dispersed, but the sense of unity and determination lingered in the air. The friends, their hearts filled with pride and hope, knew that their efforts had made a profound impact on their community, illustrating that even in the face of adversity, the power of unity and the spirit of democracy could prevail.

Part 3: Change Through Non-violence

In the days following the peaceful protest parade, the local government of Democracy Land found itself grappling with the undeniable impact of the citizens' collective voice. Initially, the town leaders were defensive, reluctant to admit that the unjust rule they had imposed was indeed threatening the very principles upon which their society was built. However, as the message of the parade continued to reverberate throughout the community, the government could no longer ignore the concerns of its people.

Recognizing the power of nonviolent resistance and the importance of upholding democratic values, the town leaders convened a series of meetings to reconsider the rule. As they deliberated, it became increasingly apparent that the citizens' concerns were valid, and that the rule must be revoked in order to preserve the harmony and fairness that defined Democracy Land. Ultimately, the government announced their decision to rescind the unjust rule, crediting the peaceful protest parade and the unwavering commitment of the citizens to the principles of democracy.

News of the government's decision spread like wildfire throughout the town, sparking spontaneous celebrations in the streets of Democracy Land. The citizens rejoiced in their victory, grateful for the peaceful resolution of the conflict and the reaffirmation of their core values. As they celebrated, they recognized the power of unity and nonviolent resistance, understanding that their peaceful approach had been instrumental in effecting change.

Lily, Alex, Maria, and Ben stood among the jubilant crowds, watching with pride as their community celebrated the fruits of their labor. The friends reflected on the journey that had led them to this moment, from their initial decision to take a stand against the unjust rule to the triumphant success of their peaceful protest parade. They had learned firsthand the importance of unity and nonviolence in effecting change in a democratic society, and they knew that they would carry these lessons with them throughout their lives.

As the celebrations continued late into the night, the four friends found themselves sharing a quiet moment together, contemplating the impact of their actions on Democracy Land. They had played a crucial role in championing the democratic principles that defined their community, proving that even in the face of adversity, the power of unity and nonviolence could triumph. And as they gazed out at the sea of smiling faces and uplifted spirits, they knew that they had made a lasting difference in the heart and soul of their beloved town.

The story of the peaceful protest parade and the friends' unwavering commitment to nonviolence and unity would become a cherished part of Democracy Land's history, inspiring generations to come. And as the citizens of the town moved forward, embracing their shared values and continuing their pursuit of fairness and freedom, they would always remember the importance of standing together in defence of their democratic ideals.

9

Story 9: The Forest of Different Opinions

Part 1: The Great Disagreement

In the charming town of Democracy Land, a group of young, enthusiastic friends known as the Little Politicians had earned a reputation for their unwavering dedication to making a positive impact in their community. Through their various adventures, they had tackled numerous challenges and learned valuable lessons about the importance of cooperation, understanding, and open-mindedness.

One day, as the Little Politicians gathered at their usual spot in the town square, they noticed a growing tension among the community members. A contentious issue had arisen, causing strong disagreements among the townspeople. The issue revolved around the future of the town's public park - some community members wished to preserve the park as a natural sanctuary for the town's flora and fauna, while others believed that it should be developed into a modern recreational facility with playgrounds, sports fields, and other amenities.

The Little Politicians were deeply concerned about the division this issue was causing. Friendships were strained, and once-amicable conversations had turned into heated debates. The friends realized that if left unresolved, the situation could cause irreparable damage to the sense of unity that had always been the foundation of their beloved community. Determined to find a solution, the Little Politicians put their heads together and decided to embark on a quest to understand the various perspectives and discover a path to common ground.

As they set out on their mission, the friends stumbled upon a mysterious place known as the Forest of Different Opinions. They had heard stories about this enchanted forest, a place where people of all backgrounds and beliefs gathered to share their perspectives, exchange ideas, and seek understanding. The Little Politicians were intrigued by the prospect of exploring this fabled forest and believed it could hold the key to resolving the conflict that was threatening to tear their community apart.

With a mix of excitement and trepidation, the Little Politicians ventured into the Forest of Different Opinions, eager to learn from the diverse array of viewpoints that awaited them. Little did they know that the journey ahead would be filled with challenges and surprises, but ultimately, it would reveal the true power of understanding and the strength that lies in diversity.

Part 2: The Quest for Common Ground

As the Little Politicians ventured deeper into the Forest of Different Opinions, they encountered an astonishingly diverse array of viewpoints and arguments. People from all walks of life and with a wide variety of opinions had gathered in this magical place to discuss and debate the issues that mattered most to them. The forest was alive with passionate conversations, heated exchanges, and thoughtful reflections.

The friends realized that if they were to find common ground on the contentious issue affecting their community, they needed to approach each conversation with open minds and open hearts. They made a conscious effort to listen carefully to every opinion, even when they differed significantly from their own beliefs. They asked questions, sought clarification, and genuinely tried to understand the concerns and motivations behind each perspective.

As the Little Politicians engaged in thoughtful conversations and debates, they began to appreciate the nuances and complexities that underpinned the issue at hand. They realized that each side had valid concerns and that there were no easy answers. The friends spent many hours reflecting on the various opinions, pondering the potential consequences of each proposed solution, and considering the long-term implications for their community.

Throughout their journey, the Little Politicians faced several challenges. Overcoming preconceived notions and biases proved to be a difficult task, as each of them held their own opinions about what was best for the community. Additionally, they discovered that finding a compromise that would satisfy everyone was no easy feat. However, they persevered, committed to the belief that the key to resolving the conflict lay in understanding and respecting the diverse perspectives that made their community so vibrant and unique.

Despite the challenges, the Little Politicians began to make progress. As they continued to explore the Forest of Different Opinions, they started to identify areas of overlap and agreement among the various viewpoints. They discovered that while the community members disagreed on the specifics, they shared a common desire to maintain the park as a welcoming and enjoyable space for all. This realization inspired the friends to search for a solution that would honour the shared values and aspirations of their fellow citizens while addressing the legitimate concerns of both sides of the debate.

Part 3: The Strength in Diversity

With renewed determination, the Little Politicians focused on the shared value they had identified in the Forest of Different Opinions: the desire for a welcoming and enjoyable park for all community members. Building on this common ground, they worked together to develop a proposal that would honour the diverse perspectives they had encountered while addressing the legitimate concerns of both sides of the debate.

The friends knew that the success of their proposal hinged on their ability to communicate the common ground they had discovered effectively. They spent countless hours refining their presentation, ensuring it was clear, persuasive, and, most importantly, respectful of the differing opinions within their community.

When the day came to present their proposal, the Little Politicians stood before their community with confidence and conviction. They shared the insights they had gained from the Forest of Different Opinions and explained how they had found a shared value that could unite the community in its efforts to resolve the contentious issue. As they unveiled their proposed solution, they emphasized the importance of embracing and understanding diverse viewpoints and working together towards a common goal.

As the community members listened to the Little Politicians' presentation, they began to see the merits of the friends' proposal. They recognized that while they might not agree on every detail, the solution offered a way to address the concerns of both sides while honouring the shared value of a welcoming and enjoyable park for all. The community members, inspired by the Little Politicians' journey and commitment to finding common ground, agreed to give the proposal a chance.

The friends' success in the Forest of Different Opinions was celebrated not only by their community but also by the diverse individuals who had shared their opinions and experiences in the magical forest. They had demonstrated the power of collaboration, understanding, and open-mindedness in overcoming disagreements and fostering unity.

As the Little Politicians looked back on their journey, they realized the invaluable lesson they had learned: the strength in diversity. It was their willingness to listen, learn, and appreciate the diverse perspectives they had encountered that had ultimately led them to find common ground and develop a solution that benefited their entire community. This experience would stay with them forever, shaping their future adventures and reinforcing their belief in the power of collaboration and the beauty of diversity.

10

Story 10: The Green Governor

Part 1: The Environmental Challenge

In the bustling town of Democracy Land, the citizens prided themselves on their close-knit community and the values they held dear. One of these values was their commitment to maintaining a healthy and sustainable environment for all inhabitants. However, as the town grew and evolved, it faced increasingly concerning environmental challenges.

Pollution from factories and vehicles filled the air with a grey haze, while rampant deforestation on the outskirts of town led to the loss of critical habitats for many species. Waste management had become a significant problem, with landfills overflowing and litter tarnishing the once-pristine streets. The citizens of Democracy Land were becoming increasingly worried about the future of their environment.

Among the worried citizens were four friends – Lily, Alex, Maria, and Ben – who often gathered to discuss the challenges facing their beloved town. They were deeply concerned about the environmental issues and felt compelled to take action. They knew that waiting for others to step up might mean waiting too long, and they were determined to make a difference.

One evening, as they sat around a table at their favourite local cafe, they decided to brainstorm and develop a community-based solution to tackle the town's environmental problems. They spent hours discussing various ideas, from organizing clean-up drives to promoting recycling programs. They knew that each small action could lead to significant change if they could rally their fellow citizens to join them.

The friends divided their tasks according to their strengths and interests. Lily, an avid gardener, took on the responsibility of researching and promoting urban green spaces. Alex, with a passion for engineering, focused on finding ways to make public transportation more environmentally friendly. Maria, a dedicated educator, decided to create awareness programs about waste management and recycling. Ben, an aspiring entrepreneur, explored innovative ideas to reduce energy consumption and promote renewable energy sources.

United by their shared concern for Democracy Land's environment, the four friends embarked on their journey to create a community-based solution to the town's environmental challenges. They knew that their commitment and hard work would be essential to preserving the environment they cherished, and they were determined to make a difference for generations to come. With a sense of purpose and enthusiasm, they set out to transform their town and protect their home.

Part 2: The Community Solution

The four friends were on a mission to bring their community-based solution to life. They spent countless hours researching and planning, diving deep into topics such as recycling, conservation, and green energy. They knew that they needed to present a comprehensive plan that would inspire their fellow citizens to join the cause and make a meaningful impact on their environment.

To reach out to their community, they organized workshops and presentations at local schools, community centres, and public spaces. They shared their ideas and initiatives, highlighting the importance of individual and collective efforts in tackling environmental challenges. They encouraged their fellow citizens to participate in clean-up drives, recycling campaigns, tree-planting activities, and energy-saving initiatives.

As word spread throughout Democracy Land, more people became engaged and committed to the environmental cause. Volunteers from all walks of life came together to help implement the friends' initiatives, demonstrating the power of collective action. The movement grew stronger with each passing day, as residents of Democracy Land saw tangible improvements in their environment.

It wasn't long before the friends' efforts caught the attention of a forward-thinking leader, known as the Green Governor. He was impressed by the dedication and passion displayed by the young activists and the impact their movement was having on the community. Recognizing the potential of their ideas, the Green Governor reached out to the friends to offer his support and resources.

With the Green Governor's backing, the friends' initiatives gained even more momentum. They secured funding for new recycling facilities, public transportation upgrades, and educational programs to promote eco-friendly practices. The Green Governor also worked to implement policies that would support and sustain the community's environmental efforts, including incentives for businesses that prioritized sustainability and regulations to protect natural habitats.

As the friends' movement continued to grow, it became clear that the power of the community had the potential to make a significant difference in Democracy Land's environmental future. The Green Governor's support had amplified their efforts, and the entire town was now engaged in the collective mission to preserve and protect their environment.

The friends were filled with a sense of accomplishment and pride as they witnessed the transformation of their town. They knew that their journey was far from over, but with the support of their fellow citizens and the guidance of the Green Governor, they were confident that they could continue to make strides towards a healthier and more sustainable future for Democracy Land.

Part 3: Protecting the Planet for Future Generations

Inspired by the friends' initiative, the Green Governor worked tirelessly to promote sustainable practices throughout Democracy Land. He believed that the efforts of Lily, Alex, Maria, and Ben were a testament to the power of grassroots activism and community engagement. With renewed vigour, the Green Governor set out to ensure that the lessons learned from the friends' movement were integrated into the fabric of the town's daily life.

The Green Governor implemented a variety of programs and policies designed to encourage sustainable practices. He introduced eco-friendly building codes, developed public transportation infrastructure, and expanded recycling programs. Furthermore, he encouraged businesses and citizens to adopt greener practices by offering incentives and educational resources to help them make more environmentally responsible choices.

As the community embraced these new practices, Democracy Land began to experience a remarkable transformation. The air became cleaner, as fewer pollutants were released into the atmosphere. Ecosystems that had once been under threat started to recover, as habitats were protected and conserved. Waste was significantly reduced, as residents and businesses participated in recycling efforts and embraced more sustainable consumption habits.

The friends watched in awe as their small initiative blossomed into a town-wide movement, bringing about profound positive changes to the environment. They understood that their success was not just due to their individual efforts, but rather a result of the collective action and responsible leadership exhibited by the entire community. It was a powerful reminder of the importance of working together to address environmental challenges.

As the friends gathered to reflect on their accomplishments, they couldn't help but feel a sense of pride and responsibility for the role they had played in protecting the planet for future generations. They knew that their journey was far from over, as there would always be new challenges to overcome and more work to be done in the quest for a sustainable future. However, they were confident that, together with their fellow citizens and the guidance of the Green Governor, they could continue to make a difference.

The story of Lily, Alex, Maria, and Ben's environmental initiative in Democracy Land serves as an inspiring example of the power of community action and responsible leadership. By working together, citizens can overcome seemingly insurmountable challenges and pave the way for a healthier, more sustainable world for generations to come. The friends' journey demonstrates that when united in a common cause, every individual can play a crucial role in protecting our planet and preserving its precious resources.

11

Story 11: The Bill-Making Quest

Part 1: The Journey to the Capitol

In the vibrant town of Democracy Land, a group of friends, known as the Little Politicians, was passionate about making a difference in their community. Lucy, the environmental activist, was always rallying for cleaner parks and more sustainable practices. Sam, the education enthusiast, tirelessly advocated for better school facilities and resources for students. Emily, a health-conscious citizen, campaigned for healthier meal options in schools and public spaces, while Max, an animal lover, devoted himself to the protection of the local wildlife.

One day, as they gathered at their usual meeting spot in Lucy's treehouse, the friends were discussing a critical issue that affected their community: the increasing pollution in the local river. They realized that the pollution was not only affecting the water quality but also harming the local wildlife and posing a threat to their fellow citizens' health. The Little Politicians felt compelled to take action.

After much deliberation, they decided to propose a bill that would address the river's pollution by regulating industrial waste disposal and encouraging more environmentally friendly practices. They knew that the journey to the Capitol and the process of passing a bill would be challenging, but they were determined to make a positive impact on their community.

Over the next few weeks, the Little Politicians prepared for their trip to the Capitol. They spent countless hours researching the legislative process, the current laws on pollution and waste disposal, and how other communities had tackled similar issues. They drafted their bill, carefully outlining the regulations they wanted to implement and the penalties for non-compliance. They also gathered supporting evidence, such as water quality reports and testimonies from local experts, to strengthen their case.

As the day of their journey to the Capitol approached, the Little Politicians were filled with excitement and anticipation. They knew that they had a challenging road ahead, but they were determined to succeed. With their bill in hand and their supporting evidence neatly organized in their folders, they set off on their journey.

The trip to the Capitol was an adventure in itself, as the friends navigated through bustling cities, quaint towns, and beautiful countryside. Along the way, they met people who shared their concern about the river's pollution and offered their support for the Little Politicians' cause. Each encounter further fuelled their determination to make a difference.

Finally, the friends arrived at the majestic Capitol, a symbol of democracy and the power of the people. They stood in awe of the grand building, knowing that within its walls, they would have the chance to change their community for the better. With their hearts full of hope and their minds focused on their mission, the Little Politicians were ready to embark on their bill-making quest.

Part 2: Navigating the Legislative Process

Upon entering the Capitol, the Little Politicians were awed by the grandeur and history of the building. They marvelled at the ornate architecture, the portraits of influential leaders from the past, and the sense of purpose that filled the air. They knew that they were standing in a place where countless important decisions had been made, and they were eager to contribute their own part to this legacy.

As they began to navigate the legislative process, the Little Politicians encountered a diverse group of individuals, including lawmakers, staffers, and lobbyists. They attended meetings, committee hearings, and debates, where they listened carefully to the discussions and learned about the intricacies of the legislative process. They quickly realized that drafting and passing a bill was no easy task, and that they would need to work tirelessly to ensure the success of their proposal.

The friends spent long hours drafting, editing, and revising their bill, taking into account the feedback they received from various stakeholders. They researched the potential impact of their proposed regulations and worked to address any concerns raised by lawmakers and industry representatives. They also learned the importance of compromise, as they negotiated with other legislators to build support for their bill.

Throughout this process, the Little Politicians faced numerous challenges and obstacles. They encountered competing interests, as some lawmakers and lobbyists advocated for different approaches to the pollution problem or sought to protect the interests of their constituents and clients. They also had to navigate the complex world of political maneuvering, where alliances were formed and broken, and deals were made behind closed doors.

Despite these challenges, the Little Politicians remained steadfast in their commitment to their cause. They knew that the health of their community and the environment was at stake, and they were determined to make a difference. They worked diligently to build support for their bill, presenting their research, sharing their passion, and appealing to the shared values of their fellow citizens.

As they made their way through the legislative process, the Little Politicians also learned valuable lessons about the importance of persistence, teamwork, and diplomacy. They discovered that change often comes slowly, but that it is possible to make a difference with determination and hard work. They also realized that by working together and building coalitions, they could overcome the obstacles they faced and achieve their goals.

As the day of the final vote on their bill approached, the Little Politicians were filled with a mixture of excitement and apprehension. They had come so far and worked so hard, but they knew that the outcome was still uncertain. With their hearts full of hope and their minds focused on their mission, they prepared for the final step in their bill-making quest.

Part 3: The Triumph of Collaboration

As the day of the final vote drew near, the Little Politicians focused their efforts on building a coalition of support for their bill. They reached out to other lawmakers, sharing their research and discussing the potential benefits of their proposal. They also connected with like-minded advocacy groups and organizations, working together to raise awareness about the issue and garner public support.

Throughout this process, the Little Politicians discovered the importance of collaboration and teamwork. They learned that by joining forces with others who shared their goals and values, they could amplify their message and increase their chances of success. They also realized that while their individual contributions were valuable, it was only through collective action that they could truly make a difference.

Finally, the day of the vote arrived. The Little Politicians gathered in the gallery of the legislative chamber, their hearts pounding with anticipation as they anxiously awaited the outcome. They watched as lawmakers debated the merits of their bill, some voicing their support while others raised concerns or suggested amendments. The friends held their breath as the speaker called for a vote, knowing that the fate of their bill – and their community – hung in the balance.

As the votes were tallied, the Little Politicians' eyes filled with tears of joy when they realized that their bill had passed. Their hard work, determination, and collaboration had paid off, resulting in a victory not only for themselves but also for the community they loved. Amidst the applause and congratulations from their fellow lawmakers, the friends embraced each other, overcome with emotion and pride in their accomplishment.

In the days that followed, the Little Politicians returned to their community, eager to share their success and the lessons they had learned. They organized a town hall meeting, where they recounted their journey and spoke about the power of civic engagement. They encouraged their neighbours to get involved in local politics and to work together to address the challenges they faced, emphasizing that everyone had a role to play in shaping the future of their community.

As they reflected on their adventure, the Little Politicians realized that they had not only made a tangible impact on their community but had also grown as individuals. They had gained a deeper understanding of the democratic process, learned the value of collaboration and teamwork, and discovered the power of their own voices. They knew that this experience had changed them forever and that they would continue to work together to make their community – and their world – a better place.

With renewed passion and a sense of purpose, the Little Politicians embarked on their next adventure, eager to tackle new challenges and make a difference wherever they went. They had learned that through collaboration and civic engagement, they could overcome even the most daunting obstacles, and they were determined to use their newfound skills and knowledge to create a brighter future for all.

12

Story 12: The Judicial Discovery

Part 1: Unraveling the Legal System

The Little Politicians had always been passionate about making a difference in their community. After learning about the legislative process, they were eager to explore another vital branch of government – the judicial branch. They believed that understanding the legal system would help them become even more effective advocates for change in their community.

One sunny afternoon, the friends gathered at their usual spot under the oak tree to discuss their new adventure. "Guys, we've learned so much about how laws are made, but we don't know much about how they're enforced and interpreted," said Maya, the group's natural-born leader. "I think it's time we delve into the legal system and see how it upholds justice."

Her friends enthusiastically agreed. They decided to embark on a journey to learn about the intricacies of the legal system, the rule of law, and the various types of courts that played a role in upholding justice. They began by researching the different branches of government, specifically focusing on the judicial branch. They learned that the judicial branch was responsible for interpreting laws and ensuring that they were applied fairly and consistently across the nation.

As the Little Politicians delved deeper into their research, they discovered the hierarchy of courts in their country, from local courts and district courts to appellate courts and the highest court, the Supreme Court. They learned about the roles and responsibilities of judges, lawyers, and juries in the legal process. They were particularly fascinated by the concept of the rule of law, which stated that all citizens, regardless of their status, were subject to the same set of laws and that the legal system was designed to protect the rights of everyone.

Eager to see the judicial process in action, the friends decided to visit a local courthouse. They contacted the court administrator and obtained permission to observe a trial. As they entered the grand building, they marvelled at the high ceilings, intricate woodwork, and solemn atmosphere that filled the space. They knew they were about to witness a crucial part of their democracy in action.

As the Little Politicians sat in the gallery, they eagerly awaited the start of the trial. They felt a sense of anticipation and curiosity, knowing that they were about to gain a deeper understanding of how the legal system worked to uphold justice in their community. Little did they know that their visit to the courthouse would be an eye-opening experience that would forever change their perspective on the importance of the judicial branch in their democracy.

Part 2: The Courtroom Conundrum

As the Little Politicians settled into their seats in the gallery, they listened intently as the court clerk announced the case that was about to commence. It was a high-stakes trial involving a prominent business owner who had been accused of fraud and embezzlement, charges that could result in a lengthy prison sentence and the forfeiture of his assets.

The friends were captivated by the gravity of the case and the serious implications it held for all parties involved. They couldn't help but feel a sense of awe as they watched the judge, clad in his traditional black robes, enter the courtroom and take his seat at the elevated bench. The lawyers, each representing one side of the case, prepared their arguments and exhibits, while the jury members, selected from the community, filed in and took their places in the jury box.

Throughout the trial, the Little Politicians observed the roles of the various participants in the courtroom. They learned that the judge was responsible for overseeing the proceedings and ensuring that the trial was conducted fairly and in accordance with the law. The prosecuting attorney was tasked with presenting evidence to prove the defendant's guilt beyond a reasonable doubt, while the defence attorney was charged with challenging the prosecution's evidence and advocating for the defendant's innocence.

The Little Politicians were particularly struck by the importance of due process and the presumption of innocence, two foundational principles of their country's legal system. They learned that every accused person was entitled to a fair and impartial trial, and that they were considered innocent until proven guilty. The burden of proof was on the prosecution, and the defence had the right to challenge and refute the evidence presented against their client.

As the trial progressed, the friends discussed the complexities of the case and the various legal arguments presented by both sides. They were fascinated by the intricate web of evidence, testimony, and legal strategy that unfolded before their eyes. They also marvelled at the skill and dedication of the lawyers, who worked tirelessly to present their cases and persuade the jury of their respective positions.

With each passing day, the suspense and tension in the courtroom grew. The Little Politicians found themselves deeply invested in the outcome of the trial, as they eagerly anticipated the jury's verdict. They realized that the justice system was not only about laws and procedures but also about human drama, emotion, and the quest for truth.

As the trial reached its climax, the prosecuting and defence attorneys delivered their impassioned closing arguments, urging the jury to carefully weigh the evidence and reach a just verdict. The jury then retired to deliberate, leaving the Little Politicians and everyone else in the courtroom anxiously awaiting their decision.

During this time, the friends couldn't help but discuss the trial and the lessons they had learned about the legal system. They debated the merits of the case and speculated about the jury's eventual decision. Through their discussions, the Little Politicians developed a newfound appreciation for the complexities and challenges of the justice system and the crucial role it played in their democracy.

As the hours turned into days, the anticipation in the courtroom reached a fever pitch. Finally, the jury returned with their verdict, and the Little Politicians held their breath as the foreperson announced the decision. Regardless of the outcome, the friends knew that they had witnessed an important and transformative event in their journey as young politicians, one that would forever shape their understanding of the law and the pursuit of justice in their community.

Part 3: Upholding Justice

The courtroom was filled with an atmosphere of suspense and anticipation as the jury finally returned to deliver their verdict. The judge instructed everyone to rise, and the Little Politicians stood alongside the others in the gallery, their hearts pounding in their chests. The foreperson of the jury addressed the court and announced the verdict: guilty. The room erupted in a mixture of gasps, sighs, and murmurs as the decision reverberated through the space.

The judge thanked the jury for their service and dismissed them before turning to the defendant, now convicted of fraud and embezzlement. He proceeded to deliver a somber and stern sentencing, detailing the consequences of the crimes committed and the impact they had on the victims, the community, and the public's trust in the business world. As the friends looked on, they realized the immense responsibility that judges and juries held in the pursuit of justice, and the ripple effect that their decisions could have on society at large.

After the trial concluded, the Little Politicians left the courthouse with a newfound understanding of the judicial process and the crucial role it played in their democracy. As they gathered at a nearby park, they excitedly discussed their experiences and the lessons they had learned. Each friend shared their thoughts and perspectives, marvelling at the intricacies of the legal system and the dedication of the professionals who worked within it.

The friends also pondered the broader implications of the trial and the importance of the justice system in upholding the rule of law and protecting the rights of all citizens. They recognized that a fair and impartial judiciary was essential in maintaining the delicate balance of power within their government and ensuring that everyone, regardless of their status or wealth, was held accountable for their actions.

As their conversation continued, the Little Politicians began to see the judicial branch as a vital pillar of their democratic society, one that safeguarded individual rights, promoted fairness, and acted as a check on the other branches of government. They realized that, just like the legislative and executive branches they had explored in their previous adventures, the judiciary was integral to the proper functioning of their democracy and the preservation of their cherished values and principles.

In the days that followed, the Little Politicians continued to reflect on their experiences in the courtroom and the lessons they had learned about the justice system. They shared their insights with their classmates, teachers, and families, eager to spread awareness about the importance of the judiciary and its role in their community. They also vowed to use their newfound knowledge to help promote justice and fairness in their own lives, whether by volunteering with local organizations, participating in civic activities, or advocating for legal reform.

As the sun began to set on their latest adventure, the friends felt a renewed sense of purpose and dedication to their democratic ideals. They knew that their journey into the world of politics was far from over, but they were confident that, armed with the knowledge and experiences they had gained, they could make a real difference in their community and beyond. And so, with their heads held high and their hearts filled with hope, the Little Politicians set off once more, eager to continue their quest to learn, grow, and make the world a better place, one adventure at a time.

13

Story 13: The Guardians of the Environment

Part 1: The Call to Action

Once again, the Little Politicians gathered at their favourite meeting spot under the old oak tree. These young, dedicated individuals were passionate about making a difference in their community. Having already experienced the inner workings of the political world, they were eager to take on a new challenge that would positively impact their world.

As the friends sat together, they couldn't help but notice the increasing environmental issues they observed both in their community and around the world. From overflowing landfills to air pollution and loss of biodiversity, the Little Politicians were growing increasingly concerned about the fate of their planet. They knew that something had to be done, and they were determined to be a part of the solution.

After a heartfelt discussion, the friends made a decision. They would take action and become the "Guardians of the Environment," vowing to promote environmental awareness and sustainable practices. With their combined knowledge, enthusiasm, and determination, they believed they could inspire change in their community and beyond.

The Little Politicians wasted no time in getting to work. They began by researching the most pressing environmental issues affecting their community and the world at large. They pored over books, articles, and documentaries to educate themselves on the complex and interconnected nature of these problems.

As they delved deeper into their research, the Little Politicians identified key areas of focus that they believed would have the greatest impact on their community. They decided to concentrate on waste reduction, clean energy, and biodiversity. These issues resonated with the friends, as they had witnessed firsthand the consequences of neglecting these critical areas.

Armed with their newfound knowledge and a clear sense of purpose, the Little Politicians were ready to embark on their mission as Guardians of the Environment. They knew that the journey ahead would be challenging, but they were more determined than ever to make a lasting difference in their world.

Part 2: Building a Green Movement

The Little Politicians knew that in order to make a real impact on the environment, they would need the support of their entire community. They began by rallying their peers, educators, and local leaders, inviting them to join their green movement. They created flyers and posters, gave presentations in classrooms, and even hosted a town hall meeting to spread their message of environmental stewardship.

Their hard work paid off, as more and more people became inspired by the Little Politicians' passion and commitment. Soon, a wave of environmental enthusiasm swept through the community, with individuals of all ages eager to contribute to the cause.

With this newfound support, the Little Politicians organized a series of community events aimed at raising awareness and promoting sustainable practices. They planned clean-up days in local parks, organized tree plantings, and held educational workshops on topics such as composting, recycling, and water conservation. These events were well-attended and sparked a sense of pride and camaraderie among community members.

Realizing the importance of engaging local businesses and organizations, the Little Politicians reached out to them to discuss ways in which they could implement eco-friendly initiatives. They collaborated with local grocery stores to set up recycling programs, worked with schools to introduce energy-efficient upgrades, and partnered with environmental groups to promote the use of renewable energy sources.

But the Little Politicians didn't stop there. They knew that in order to make a lasting impact, they needed to advocate for sustainable policies and practices at the local government level. They attended city council meetings and presented their research, emphasizing the importance of long-term planning and environmental stewardship.

They proposed the creation of a sustainability committee, which would work to integrate environmentally friendly practices into local government operations and decision-making processes. The Little Politicians also encouraged the adoption of policies that would support the expansion of green spaces, promote clean transportation options, and incentivize energy efficiency improvements in homes and businesses.

Through their tireless efforts, the Little Politicians began to see their community transform. The green movement they had started was taking hold, and the positive effects of their work were becoming increasingly evident. They knew, however, that the journey was far from over, and they remained committed to their mission as Guardians of the Environment.

Part 3: Inspiring Sustainable Change

As the Little Politicians' green movement gained momentum, their community began to see tangible, positive changes. Parks and public spaces became cleaner and greener, while businesses and households adopted more sustainable practices. Recycling rates soared, and many people started making environmentally conscious choices in their daily lives, from conserving water to using reusable bags and containers.

The Little Politicians realized that their message was resonating with their community, and they felt inspired to expand their movement beyond their hometown. They reached out to other youth groups, environmental organizations, and schools in neighbouring towns, hoping to share their story and learn from others' experiences.

They attended conferences and participated in online forums, exchanging ideas and strategies for promoting environmental awareness and sustainability. They discovered that their movement was part of a larger, global effort to protect the environment, and they felt a sense of camaraderie with other change makers who shared their passion.

With each new connection and partnership, the Little Politicians' influence grew, and their movement began to inspire sustainable change on a larger scale. Their innovative projects and initiatives were highlighted in local and regional media outlets, further spreading the message of environmental stewardship.

The Little Politicians couldn't help but celebrate their accomplishments. They organized a community-wide event to showcase the progress they had made, inviting everyone who had been part of their journey to join in the festivities. They set up informational booths, screened documentaries on environmental topics, and organized workshops for children and adults alike.

During the event, the friends took a moment to reflect on their journey as Guardians of the Environment. They realized that their success was not only a result of their own determination and hard work, but also the collective efforts of their community. They understood that everyone had a role to play in preserving the environment, and that change was possible when people worked together toward a common goal.

As the sun set on their celebration, the Little Politicians knew that their work was far from over. They were more committed than ever to their mission of promoting environmental awareness and sustainability.

They felt a renewed sense of purpose, driven by the knowledge that their efforts were making a difference in their community and beyond.

Together, the Little Politicians pledged to continue their work as Guardians of the Environment, knowing that the future of their planet depended on the collective action and environmental stewardship of their generation and those to come.

14

Story 14: The Pioneers of Innovation

Part 1: Imagining a Better Future

The Little Politicians were a group of young, dedicated individuals passionate about making a difference in their community. They believed that through hard work, determination, and collaboration, they could help create positive change in the world around them. Each of them had their own strengths and skills, but together, they formed a formidable team.

One day, as the friends were gathered in their favourite meeting spot, they began discussing the rapid advances in technology and innovation. They marvelled at how these forces had the potential to improve the lives of their fellow citizens in a multitude of ways. From faster transportation to better healthcare, the possibilities seemed endless. As they talked, they couldn't help but wonder how they could harness this power to better their own community.

Inspired by the potential of these cutting-edge innovations and ideas, the Little Politicians decided to embark on a new mission: to research and explore groundbreaking advancements with the goal of finding ways to apply them to their community. They understood that in order to create lasting change, they needed to stay informed about the latest developments in various fields and learn how they could be implemented locally.

As the friends began their research, they started discussing the various areas in which their community could potentially benefit from innovation. They identified several key sectors that they believed were ripe for improvement, such as infrastructure, education, healthcare, and public services.

In the realm of infrastructure, the Little Politicians believed that advancements in clean energy, efficient transportation systems, and sustainable building materials could revolutionize the way their community functioned. They discussed the possibility of implementing solar-powered streetlights, electric buses, and bike lanes to promote greener transportation alternatives.

When it came to education, the friends considered the potential of e-learning platforms, virtual classrooms, and cutting-edge teaching methods to enhance the learning experience for students in their community. They believed that by integrating technology into the education system, they could help bridge the digital divide and prepare students for the future.

In healthcare, the Little Politicians recognized the promise of telemedicine, personalized treatments, and advanced medical devices to improve the quality of care for their fellow citizens. They discussed how these innovations could potentially make healthcare more accessible and affordable, especially for those in underserved areas.

Finally, they turned their attention to public services, considering the potential of smart city technology, data-driven decision-making, and advanced communication systems to streamline and improve the efficiency of local government operations.

As the Little Politicians delved deeper into their research and discussed the various ways in which innovation could transform their community, they knew they were on the cusp of something truly remarkable. With each new idea and discovery, their excitement grew, and they became more determined than ever to bring these advancements to their hometown. Little did they know that this journey would lead them on an incredible adventure, one that would teach them invaluable lessons about the power of imagination, collaboration, and determination.

Part 2: The Pursuit of Progress

As the Little Politicians continued their mission to explore the world of innovation, they began delving deeper into various fields that held the promise of transforming their community. They focused their attention on areas such as renewable energy, artificial intelligence, and biotechnology, eager to learn about the latest advancements and how they could be applied to their hometown.

In their pursuit of progress, the friends reached out to a diverse group of individuals who were at the forefront of these groundbreaking fields. They met with inventors who were developing cutting-edge renewable energy technologies, entrepreneurs who were harnessing the power of artificial intelligence to create smarter cities, and researchers who were pushing the boundaries of biotechnology to revolutionize healthcare.

Through their interactions with these trailblazers, the Little Politicians gained invaluable insights into the world of innovation. They learned about the challenges and obstacles faced by those who dared to dream big and push the boundaries of what was possible. They heard stories of setbacks, failures, and moments of doubt, but also of perseverance, determination, and eventual triumph.

These encounters inspired the Little Politicians to think about how they could contribute to the pursuit of progress themselves. They realized that while they might not be inventors or researchers, they had their own unique skills and perspectives that could help drive innovation in their community.

As the friends began brainstorming ideas, they started to see the potential for their own contributions. They imagined a future where solar panels adorned every rooftop, providing clean energy to power their homes and schools. They envisioned a world where artificial intelligence helped optimize traffic flow, reducing congestion and pollution. And they saw the possibilities of biotechnology, where personalized medicine and gene editing could help eradicate diseases and improve the quality of life for their fellow citizens.

Working together, the Little Politicians developed a series of proposals aimed at promoting innovation in their community. They researched potential funding sources and partnerships, drafted presentations to pitch their ideas to local leaders, and reached out to experts for advice and guidance.

As they worked on their proposals, they encountered their fair share of challenges and setbacks. There were times when they felt discouraged or overwhelmed by the complexity of the issues they were trying to address. But each time they faced an obstacle, they remembered the stories of perseverance and determination they had heard from the innovators they had met. These stories fuelled their resolve to keep pushing forward and working towards their goal of creating a better future for their community.

With each new idea and innovation, the Little Politicians grew more confident in their ability to make a difference. They knew that progress was not easy or straightforward, but they also understood that through collaboration, creativity, and determination, they could help shape the world of tomorrow. And as they embarked on this exciting journey, they knew they were not alone; they were part of a community of dreamers, doers, and change makers, all united by a shared vision of a brighter future.

Part 3: Shaping Tomorrow's World

The day finally arrived when the Little Politicians were ready to present their ideas and innovations to the local leaders and decision-makers. They had meticulously prepared their proposals, rehearsed their presentations, and armed themselves with facts and figures to support their arguments. As they stood in front of the city council, they felt a mix of excitement and nervousness, knowing that this moment could be a turning point for their community.

The friends took turns presenting their proposals, each of them speaking passionately about the potential benefits of their chosen innovation. They explained how solar panels could make their community more energy-independent and environmentally friendly, how artificial intelligence could streamline public services and improve infrastructure, and how biotechnology could revolutionize healthcare and save lives.

As they spoke, they could see that the decision-makers were taking their ideas seriously. The council members asked thoughtful questions and engaged in spirited debates, weighing the costs and benefits of each proposal. It was clear that the Little Politicians had succeeded in capturing their attention and making a strong case for change.

But the friends knew that gaining the support of the local leaders was only part of the battle. They understood that they also needed to rally their community behind their vision of a better future. And so, they embarked on a campaign to raise awareness about the potential benefits of their proposed innovations.

The Little Politicians organized community meetings, wrote letters to the local newspaper, and created social media campaigns to share their ideas with their peers, educators, and fellow citizens. They held fundraisers to support the implementation of their proposals and enlisted the help of local businesses and organizations to amplify their message.

As the weeks and months passed, the Little Politicians saw their hard work starting to pay off. One by one, their ideas were gradually adopted by their community. Solar panels began to appear on rooftops, artificial intelligence was integrated into the local traffic system, and biotechnology advancements started to make a difference in the lives of patients at the local hospital.

With each innovation implemented, the Little Politicians witnessed the positive impact their ideas had on the community. They saw how their efforts led to a cleaner environment, more efficient public services, and better healthcare for their neighbours. And as they watched their community transform, they couldn't help but feel a tremendous sense of pride and accomplishment.

In the end, the friends gathered together to reflect on their journey as Pioneers of Innovation. They marvelled at how far they had come, from merely imagining a better future to actively shaping it. They recognized the power of imagination, collaboration, and determination in making a lasting difference in the lives of those around them.

As they looked ahead to the challenges that still lay before them, the Little Politicians knew that they were more than capable of overcoming them. They had learned that by working together, dreaming big, and never giving up, they could truly shape tomorrow's world and create a better future for all.

15

Story 15: The Champions of Education

Part 1: Recognizing the Power of Knowledge

The Little Politicians, a group of enthusiastic and dedicated young friends, were always on a mission to make a difference in their community. Amy, the natural-born leader, was resourceful and had a gift for bringing people together. Ben, the thinker, was always full of creative ideas and solutions to problems. Cassie, the social butterfly, was excellent at spreading the word and rallying support. And Dan, the hard worker, was always ready to roll up his sleeves and get things done.

One day, while discussing ways to create a better future for their community, the friends had an epiphany. They realized that the key to a brighter future lay in the power of education and knowledge. Without a strong educational foundation, the children in their community would struggle to reach their full potential and contribute positively to society. The Little Politicians knew that if they wanted to make a lasting impact, they had to focus on improving the educational opportunities available to every child in their community.

With a newfound sense of purpose, the Little Politicians set out on a fact-finding mission. They began by researching the current state of education in their community, from the quality of the schools and the resources available to the teachers and students, to the existing programs and extracurricular activities. They interviewed teachers, administrators, parents, and students, asking them about their experiences and gathering their insights on what could be improved.

Through their research, the Little Politicians identified several areas in need of improvement. They found that some schools in their community were struggling to provide adequate resources and support for their students, particularly those from low-income families. They also discovered that there was a significant disparity in the quality of education between schools in different neighbourhoods. Furthermore, they learned that many students were not receiving the support they needed to excel academically and develop essential life skills.

Armed with this information, the Little Politicians began brainstorming potential solutions to address the challenges they had uncovered. They knew that they couldn't solve every problem overnight, but they were determined to make a difference, one step at a time. Together, they vowed to become the Champions of Education in their community, fighting for a better future for every child. And so, their journey began.

Part 2: Empowering the Next Generation

The Little Politicians, now fully committed to their roles as Champions of Education, began the hard work of advocating for better educational resources, programs, and facilities in their community. They knew that the key to success lay in engaging parents, educators, and local leaders, so they reached out to various stakeholders, sharing their findings and discussing potential solutions.

One of their first initiatives was to organize a town hall meeting, inviting parents, teachers, school administrators, and local government representatives to discuss the current state of education in their community. At the meeting, the Little Politicians presented their research and ideas for improvement, sparking a lively and constructive dialogue among the attendees. They emphasized the need for collaboration and community involvement, encouraging everyone to take an active role in supporting education.

As they continued to build support, the Little Politicians organized various events and initiatives to raise awareness about the importance of education. They partnered with local schools to establish tutoring programs, matching high-achieving students with those in need of academic support. They also launched a literacy drive, collecting donated books and organizing reading clubs to promote the joy of reading among children of all ages. Additionally, they held community workshops on topics such as digital literacy, financial education, and effective study habits, helping parents and students alike to develop essential skills for success.

Despite their determination and hard work, the Little Politicians faced numerous challenges along the way. Funding constraints meant that they often had to get creative with their initiatives, seeking grants, donations, and in-kind contributions from local businesses and organizations. Bureaucratic hurdles sometimes slowed their progress, as they navigated the complexities of local government policies and regulations. They also encountered resistance to change from those who were skeptical of their ideas or unwilling to invest time and resources in improving education.

However, the Little Politicians refused to let these obstacles deter them. They remained focused on their mission, drawing strength from the knowledge that their efforts were making a difference in the lives of the children in their community. They continued to work tirelessly, rallying support, and forging partnerships with like-minded individuals and organizations. They found that when they faced challenges, their collective passion, creativity, and perseverance allowed them to overcome even the most daunting obstacles.

Through their advocacy, the Little Politicians gradually began to see positive changes in their community. Schools started receiving additional resources and support, enabling them to better serve their students. New programs and initiatives were introduced, providing children with a more well-rounded education and opportunities for personal growth. Parents and educators became more engaged and proactive, working together to create a supportive and nurturing learning environment for all children.

The journey was not an easy one, but the Little Politicians knew that the future of their community depended on their ability to empower the next generation through education. They understood that every child deserved the chance to learn, grow, and thrive, and they were determined to do everything in their power to make that dream a reality.

Part 3: The Gift of Opportunity

The Little Politicians' hard work and dedication began to pay off, as their efforts to improve education in their community gained traction. New educational programs were implemented in schools, providing students with a more diverse range of learning experiences. Funding was secured for better resources, including updated textbooks, technology, and classroom materials, thanks to the friends' tireless efforts to secure grants and donations.

Community-wide support for their mission grew, as parents, educators, and local leaders witnessed the positive changes that were taking place. The Little Politicians' passion for education proved infectious, inspiring others to get involved and contribute to the cause. Schools became hubs of activity, with parents volunteering their time and expertise to support various initiatives, and local businesses offering resources and sponsorships.

The impact of the Little Politicians' efforts on the lives of the children in their community was nothing short of transformative. Students who had once struggled academically began to flourish, thanks to the additional support and resources provided by the friends' initiatives. Children who had lacked access to extracurricular activities and enrichment programs now had opportunities to explore their interests and develop their talents. The gift of opportunity was evident in every aspect of their education, empowering them to reach their full potential and dream big.

As the friends witnessed the fruits of their labor, they couldn't help but feel a sense of pride and accomplishment. They knew that their efforts had made a lasting difference in the lives of their community's youngest members, providing them with the tools and opportunities they needed to succeed. They celebrated their achievements with a community-wide event, inviting students, parents, educators, and local leaders to come together and share in the joy of their collective success.

The Little Politicians took the opportunity to reflect on the power of education and the gift of opportunity. They realized that by investing in the next generation, they were not only helping individual children but also strengthening the fabric of their community as a whole. They understood that the knowledge and skills acquired through education were gifts that would last a lifetime, opening doors to new possibilities and empowering children to create a brighter future for themselves and their society.

As the sun set on their celebration, the Little Politicians knew that their work was far from over. There would always be new challenges to face, new opportunities to seize, and new dreams to nurture. But they had come a long way since they first embarked on their mission to champion education, and they were more determined than ever to continue their journey. The Little Politicians had become true agents of change in their community, and they were ready to face whatever adventures lay ahead, united in their belief in the power of education and the gift of opportunity.

16

Story 16: The Dynamic Diplomats

Part 1: Fostering International Relations

The Little Politicians were a group of friends who shared a passion for learning and making a difference in their community. They had already embarked on numerous adventures, tackling issues such as education, the environment, and innovation. Now, they were eager to learn about the wider world and the role of diplomacy in maintaining peace and cooperation among nations.

One day, during their weekly meeting at the local library, the friends decided to research international relations and diplomacy. Their goal was to understand how they could contribute to fostering peace and collaboration among nations. Together, they delved into the history of diplomacy, learning about the intricate world of ambassadors, embassies, and the delicate dance of international negotiations.

As they researched, the Little Politicians became fascinated by the various international organizations that worked tirelessly to address global issues such as poverty, climate change, and human rights. They learned about the United Nations, the World Health Organization, and the International Monetary Fund, among others. These organizations, they discovered, played a crucial role in maintaining peace and promoting cooperation among countries.

One day, the friends came across an opportunity that they couldn't pass up: a local Model United Nations (MUN) conference was taking place soon. They knew that attending the conference would give them a chance to experience diplomacy in action and learn about the challenges faced by diplomats from around the world.

The Little Politicians eagerly signed up for the MUN conference, selecting different countries to represent and researching their assigned nations' histories, cultures, and political stances. They spent weeks preparing for the conference, practicing their debating skills and learning about the proper protocols and procedures for diplomatic negotiations.

Finally, the day of the MUN conference arrived. The Little Politicians dressed in their most professional attire and headed to the conference venue, their hearts pounding with excitement and anticipation. Upon entering the conference hall, they were amazed by the diversity of the attendees, who had come from schools all over the region to participate.

Throughout the conference, the Little Politicians participated in heated debates and discussions on various global issues, such as climate change, nuclear disarmament, and human trafficking. They learned to listen carefully to the perspectives of others and to communicate their own ideas clearly and persuasively. They also discovered the importance of compromise and collaboration in reaching consensus on complex and contentious issues.

As the conference progressed, the friends experienced firsthand the challenges faced by diplomats in the real world. They encountered language barriers, cultural differences, and conflicting interests that sometimes made it difficult to find common ground. Yet, they also witnessed moments of incredible unity and cooperation, as delegates from diverse backgrounds came together to work towards a shared goal.

By the end of the MUN conference, the Little Politicians had gained a profound appreciation for the role of diplomacy in maintaining peace and fostering cooperation among nations. They knew that their experience at the conference was just the beginning of a lifelong journey to promote understanding and collaboration in an increasingly interconnected world.

Part 2: Navigating Cultural Differences

The Little Politicians' experience at the Model United Nations conference had opened their eyes to the vast diversity of cultures and perspectives in the world. They realized that understanding and respecting cultural differences was essential for successful diplomatic relations and fostering international cooperation.

Eager to continue their diplomatic journey, the friends decided to learn more about the customs, traditions, and values of various countries. They recognized that open-mindedness and cultural sensitivity were crucial in bridging divides and promoting understanding among nations. The Little Politicians set out to deepen their knowledge of world cultures, researching the history, geography, and societal norms of different countries.

As they delved into their studies, the friends began to appreciate the richness and complexity of the world's cultures. They learned about the nuances of etiquette and manners, the significance of religious beliefs and practices, and the importance of language in shaping thought and communication. The Little Politicians recognized that they needed to develop their cultural intelligence to become effective diplomats.

To practice their diplomatic skills and better understand other cultures, the Little Politicians began engaging in cultural exchanges with their peers from around the world. They connected with students from various countries online, joining international forums and discussion groups, and participating in video conferences. They also had the opportunity to host and attend cultural events in their community, where they met people from different backgrounds and shared their own experiences and perspectives.

Through these cultural exchanges, the friends learned invaluable lessons about the importance of empathy, active listening, and respectful dialogue. They also faced challenges as they navigated cultural differences, such as language barriers, etiquette, and conflicting perspectives on global issues.

One day, the Little Politicians participated in an online debate about climate change with students from several countries. They quickly realized that while they shared the same goal of protecting the environment, their views on how to achieve this goal differed greatly. Some students argued for more stringent regulations and international agreements, while others prioritized economic development and technological innovation.

As the debate became heated, the Little Politicians faced the challenge of balancing their own convictions with the need for diplomatic tact and cultural sensitivity. They acknowledged the validity of different perspectives and sought to find common ground. By doing so, they were able to foster a constructive dialogue that highlighted the importance of global collaboration in addressing climate change.

The friends also encountered difficulties in overcoming language barriers and understanding unfamiliar customs and traditions. They experienced moments of confusion and embarrassment, such as when they accidentally offended someone by using the wrong greeting or committing a cultural faux pas. However, these experiences taught the Little Politicians the importance of humility, patience, and adaptability in the complex world of diplomacy.

Throughout their journey, the Little Politicians continued to refine their diplomatic skills, learning from their successes and failures. They became more adept at navigating cultural differences and fostering understanding among diverse groups of people. The friends were proud of the progress they had made and were committed to promoting cultural exchange and understanding in their community and beyond.

As the Little Politicians reflected on their experiences, they recognized that their newfound diplomatic skills would serve them well in their future adventures. They knew that the ability to navigate cultural differences and foster cooperation among nations was essential for creating a more peaceful and interconnected world. With renewed determination, the friends embarked on the next chapter of their journey as the Dynamic Diplomats, ready to face the challenges and opportunities that lay ahead.

Part 3: Building Bridges Across Borders

The Little Politicians, now embracing their roles as Dynamic Diplomats, were determined to apply their newfound knowledge and skills to promote understanding and collaboration between people of different cultures and nations. They recognized that building bridges across borders would play a crucial role in fostering peace and cooperation in an increasingly interconnected world.

To this end, the friends began organizing events and initiatives that brought together diverse groups of people. They started by planning a cultural festival in their community, inviting people from various countries and backgrounds to share their customs, traditions, and food. The Little Politicians believed that by celebrating different cultures, they could encourage empathy and understanding among their fellow citizens.

The cultural festival was a resounding success, drawing large crowds and fostering a lively atmosphere of curiosity and camaraderie. People of all ages and backgrounds mingled, learning about each other's cultures through music, dance, art, and cuisine. The Little Politicians were delighted to see friendships form and stereotypes fade away as their community embraced the spirit of the festival.

Encouraged by the success of the cultural festival, the friends decided to expand their efforts by organizing international forums and student exchange programs. They reached out to schools and organizations around the world, building connections and fostering dialogue on important global issues such as climate change, human rights, and economic development. The Little Politicians believed that by engaging young people in these discussions, they could empower the next generation of global citizens and leaders.

The international forums provided a platform for students from different countries to exchange ideas, challenge assumptions, and collaborate on solutions to shared challenges. As these young people interacted, they discovered that despite their diverse backgrounds, they had much in common and could learn from each other's experiences and perspectives.

The student exchange programs, meanwhile, allowed participants to immerse themselves in different cultures, living and studying abroad for a period of time. The Little Politicians saw firsthand how these experiences broadened the horizons of the participants and enriched their understanding of the world. They also noticed how the host communities benefited from the presence of these international students, who brought fresh ideas and unique perspectives to their classrooms and neighbourhoods.

Throughout their journey as Dynamic Diplomats, the Little Politicians witnessed the positive impact of their efforts. Friendships and alliances were forged across borders, as people learned to appreciate the richness and diversity of the world's cultures. The friends saw how their initiatives created a ripple effect, inspiring others to join the cause and promoting a greater understanding of cultural differences.

As the Little Politicians reflected on their accomplishments, they felt a deep sense of pride and satisfaction. They had successfully navigated the complex world of diplomacy and international relations, fostering unity and cooperation among people of different cultures and nations. They recognized the power of diplomacy, cultural understanding, and unity in promoting peace and cooperation in an increasingly interconnected world.

However, the friends also understood that their work was far from over. They knew that there would always be new challenges to face, and new opportunities to build bridges across borders. The Little Politicians were determined to continue their journey as Dynamic Diplomats, using their skills and passion to create a more peaceful, understanding, and united world. They looked forward to the adventures that awaited them, knowing that together, they could make a lasting difference in the lives of people around the globe.

17

Story 17: The Courageous Campaigners

Part 1: The Call to Lead

In the quiet town of Democracy Land, the Little Politicians were well-known for their passion and dedication to making a difference in their community. Having already tackled various issues, from the environment to education, the group of friends had developed a strong sense of civic responsibility and a desire to enact positive change.

One day, as they gathered in their favourite meeting spot under the large oak tree in the town square, the Little Politicians decided it was time to take their commitment to the next level. Inspired by their previous experiences in promoting change and their belief in the power of democracy, they made a collective decision to participate in the upcoming local elections. They hoped that by running for office, they could directly influence the policies and actions that shaped their community.

Excited about their new mission, the Little Politicians began to research the election process. They delved into the intricacies of voter registration, understanding the importance of encouraging their fellow citizens to make their voices heard at the polls. They studied the art of campaigning, learning about the various methods and strategies used by candidates to connect with voters and promote their ideas. And, most importantly, they familiarized themselves with the responsibilities of various local government positions, such as city council members, school board representatives, and even the town mayor.

After days of careful research and discussion, the Little Politicians selected the positions they would run for, each choosing a role that aligned with their passions and areas of expertise. For instance, Sophia, who was passionate about education, decided to run for a seat on the school board. Meanwhile, Liam, a natural leader with a gift for public speaking, set his sights on becoming the town mayor.

With their positions chosen, the Little Politicians set to work developing their campaign platforms. They held brainstorming sessions, discussing the issues that mattered most to them and their community. They debated solutions to problems like traffic congestion, limited access to quality healthcare, and the need for more green spaces in the town. By the end of their discussions, each Little Politician had a clear vision of the changes they wanted to bring to Democracy Land.

As their campaigns began to take shape, the Little Politicians felt a mixture of excitement and nervousness. They knew they were embarking on a challenging journey, but their determination to make a difference in their community fuelled their resolve. With their campaign platforms ready and their eyes on the prize, the Little Politicians eagerly prepared for the adventure that lay ahead.

Part 2: Running for Office

The Little Politicians' campaigns were now in full swing, and they dove headfirst into the world of politics. They knew that in order to succeed, they had to connect with the citizens of Democracy Land, so they embarked on a series of campaign activities to make their voices heard.

Armed with their campaign materials and a strong sense of determination, the Little Politicians began door-to-door canvassing. They walked through the neighbourhoods of Democracy Land, knocking on doors, introducing themselves, and discussing their ideas with the residents. Each conversation provided them with valuable insights into the concerns and priorities of their fellow citizens, helping them tailor their platforms to better address the community's needs.

In addition to canvassing, the Little Politicians attended numerous community events, such as town hall meetings, neighbourhood gatherings, and local festivals. They seized every opportunity to engage with the public, listen to their stories, and share their vision for a brighter future in Democracy Land. During these events, they handed out flyers, delivered speeches, and even participated in lively debates with other candidates.

Throughout their campaigns, the Little Politicians faced numerous challenges. Time management was a constant struggle, as they juggled their schoolwork, extracurricular activities, and personal lives alongside their campaign responsibilities. They also had to deal with criticism from opponents and skeptical voters, learning to respond with grace, diplomacy, and a focus on their own message. Setbacks, such as losing a key endorsement or a disappointing showing in a debate, tested their resilience, but they refused to let these obstacles deter them.

Despite the difficulties, the Little Politicians never wavered in their support for one another. They pooled their resources, shared their experiences, and provided encouragement during the toughest moments of the campaign. They brainstormed ideas together, practiced their speeches in front of each other, and cheered one another on at debates and events. The camaraderie among the friends was a testament to their shared commitment to making a difference in their community.

As the campaign progressed, the Little Politicians grew in many ways. Their understanding of the issues affecting Democracy Land deepened, and they became more adept at articulating their ideas and solutions. They honed their communication skills, learning to navigate the delicate balance between promoting their platforms and listening to the needs of the people they hoped to represent. And, perhaps most importantly, they gained a greater appreciation for the complexities of politics and the responsibilities that come with being a public servant.

With Election Day fast approaching, the Little Politicians knew that win or lose, their journey as candidates had been a transformative experience. They were ready to face the final stage of their campaign with courage, conviction, and an unwavering commitment to the people of Democracy Land.

Part 3: The Triumph of Democracy

Election day finally arrived in Democracy Land, and the Little Politicians could feel the excitement and anticipation in the air. They knew that their community's future was in the hands of its citizens, and they eagerly awaited the outcome of the elections. As the polls opened, the friends spent the day encouraging their fellow citizens to cast their votes, emphasizing the power of each individual's voice in shaping the direction of their community.

As the polls closed and the votes were tallied, the Little Politicians gathered together to await the election results. The atmosphere was tense, but they took the opportunity to reflect on their journey and the lessons they had learned along the way. They discussed the importance of leadership, the challenges of democracy, and the value of civic engagement. Regardless of the outcome, they knew that they had grown as individuals and as a team, better equipped to serve their community in various capacities.

When the results finally came in, a mix of joy, pride, and determination filled the room. Some of the Little Politicians had won their elections, and they were overjoyed at the opportunity to serve their community in an official capacity. Their hard work, dedication, and passion had paid off, and they were eager to make a positive impact as elected officials.

For those who didn't win, the initial disappointment was quickly replaced with resolve. They knew that while they may not have been elected to office, they could still contribute to their community in other ways. Their journey had taught them the power of grassroots activism, and they vowed to continue their efforts to improve Democracy Land, whether through volunteering, advocacy, or other forms of civic engagement.

The Little Politicians came together to celebrate their achievements, knowing that their campaigns had been a triumph of democracy. They had given a voice to the people of Democracy Land, engaged with their fellow citizens, and inspired others to take an active role in their community. Win or lose, they had demonstrated the power of people in shaping the future of their community.

As they looked forward to the next chapter of their lives, the Little Politicians knew that their experiences as candidates had prepared them for whatever challenges and opportunities lay ahead. They were proud of their journey and the difference they had made in Democracy Land. And, most importantly, they were ready to continue their adventures as dedicated citizens, committed to the ideals of democracy and the betterment of their beloved community.

18

Story 18: The Pillars of the Community

Part 1: Identifying Local Needs

The sun rose on another beautiful day in Democracy Land, as the Little Politicians, a group of dedicated and passionate friends, prepared for another day of making a difference in their community. They had already embarked on numerous adventures, each one teaching them valuable lessons about democracy, leadership, and the importance of civic engagement. This time, they decided to focus on assessing the needs of their local community and identifying areas that required attention.

The friends – Sarah, Alex, Lucy, Ethan, and Jake – gathered at their favourite meeting spot, the local library, to discuss their plan of action. They knew that in order to make a real difference, they needed to understand the most pressing concerns of their fellow citizens. They decided to conduct surveys, attend community meetings, and engage in discussions with various stakeholders to gather information and identify key issues.

Armed with clipboards, pens, and an unwavering determination, the Little Politicians split up and ventured into different parts of their community. They spoke with residents, local business owners, and even government officials to gain a comprehensive understanding of the challenges their community faced. They also attended town hall meetings and participated in neighbourhood association gatherings, listening intently to the concerns and suggestions of their fellow community members.

After weeks of research and countless conversations, the Little Politicians reconvened at the library to share their findings. They had discovered that their community faced a range of issues, including public safety, infrastructure, and community development. The friends knew that they couldn't tackle all of these issues at once, so they decided to prioritize them and form action plans to address each one in turn.

Public safety was identified as the most pressing issue, as several community members had expressed concerns about the lack of streetlights in certain areas and the need for a more visible police presence. Infrastructure came in as a close second, with residents complaining about poorly maintained roads, cracked sidewalks, and outdated public facilities. Lastly, community development was highlighted as an area for improvement, with suggestions for more community events, increased support for local businesses, and better access to public services.

With their priorities set, the Little Politicians rolled up their sleeves and prepared to take action. They were determined to work together and rally their community to address these pressing needs and make their beloved Democracy Land an even better place to live.

Part 2: Uniting for a Common Goal

The Little Politicians knew that to bring about meaningful change, they needed the support of their community, local businesses, and government officials. They were determined to unite everyone for the common goal of improving their community.

They began by reaching out to community members, sharing their findings and proposed action plans. They organized neighbourhood meetings, inviting local residents to discuss their ideas and voice their concerns. The friends listened carefully to everyone's opinions, ensuring that everyone felt heard and valued.

Next, they approached local businesses, explaining how improvements in public safety, infrastructure, and community development would benefit them as well. They were pleased to find many businesses eager to contribute, offering financial support, resources, and expertise to help with various projects and initiatives.

Finally, they met with government officials, presenting their well-researched action plans and emphasizing the benefits of investing in their community. The officials were impressed by the Little Politicians' dedication and thoroughness, and they agreed to work together to address the identified needs.

With the support of their community, local businesses, and government officials, the Little Politicians began organizing workshops and events to facilitate collaboration and cooperation among stakeholders. They held public safety workshops, where they taught residents about the importance of neighbourhood watch programs and shared tips for improving personal safety. They also coordinated park clean-ups, encouraging community members to take pride in their shared green spaces and fostering a sense of collective responsibility.

To address infrastructure issues, the friends organized volunteer-driven projects to fix cracked sidewalks and clean up litter-strewn streets. They also worked closely with local government officials to secure funding for the repair of damaged roads and the improvement of public facilities.

However, the journey was not without its challenges. The Little Politicians faced differing opinions among community members, with some prioritizing certain projects over others. They learned the importance of compromise and collaboration, finding ways to accommodate the diverse needs and concerns of their community.

Resource constraints also presented a significant challenge, as there were limited funds and materials available for their various initiatives. The friends had to think creatively and strategically, finding ways to stretch their resources and maximize their impact. They organized fundraisers and sought donations from local businesses, demonstrating their resourcefulness and commitment to their cause.

Logistical obstacles were another hurdle the Little Politicians had to overcome. Coordinating large-scale projects and events required significant planning and organization, which tested the friends' leadership skills and adaptability. They divided responsibilities among themselves, ensuring that each task was completed efficiently and effectively.

Despite these challenges, the Little Politicians persevered, driven by their unwavering commitment to their community and their shared vision for a brighter future. They understood that working together and uniting for a common goal was the key to overcoming obstacles and achieving success.

As they watched their community transform before their eyes, the Little Politicians felt a deep sense of pride and accomplishment. They knew that their efforts had made a lasting difference in the lives of their fellow citizens and that they had demonstrated the power of collaboration, cooperation, and unity in achieving meaningful change.

Part 3: The Power of Collaboration

As the Little Politicians' collaborative efforts began to bear fruit, they witnessed tangible improvements in their community. Public safety had improved, thanks to the neighbourhood watch programs they had initiated, and residents felt safer and more secure in their daily lives. Infrastructure enhancements, such as repaired sidewalks, cleaner streets, and better-maintained parks, contributed to a more pleasant and inviting environment for all.

The various projects and initiatives also had a profound impact on the relationships within the community. Neighbours who had previously been strangers now worked side by side to achieve a common goal, forging new friendships and deepening existing bonds. Local businesses and government officials recognized the value of investing in their community, and they continued to support the Little Politicians' efforts. The sense of unity and shared purpose among the various stakeholders was palpable, and the community flourished as a result.

The friends took the time to reflect on their experiences and the lessons they had learned throughout their journey. They understood the power of collaboration, teamwork, and collective action in effecting positive change. They realized that by bringing diverse perspectives and resources together, they could accomplish far more than they ever could have individually.

The Little Politicians also recognized the importance of communication, listening, and compromise in maintaining harmony and cooperation among their community members. They had learned to appreciate the value of each person's unique contributions and to respect the differing opinions and priorities of their fellow citizens. This newfound wisdom would serve them well in their future endeavours, as they continued to work together to make their community an even better place to live.

As they celebrated their accomplishments, the friends felt a profound sense of pride in their role as pillars of the community. They had shown their fellow citizens the power of collaboration and the remarkable impact that a group of dedicated individuals could have when they united for a common cause.

Although they knew that their work was far from over, the Little Politicians were energized and inspired by their achievements. They were committed to continuing their efforts, working together to identify and address new challenges as they arose, and making a positive difference in the lives of their fellow citizens.

In their hearts, the friends understood that they had not only transformed their community, but they had also transformed themselves. They had become stronger leaders, more compassionate neighbours, and more effective advocates for positive change. The lessons they had learned about the power of collaboration would stay with them for the rest of their lives, guiding them as they continued their journey as the Little Politicians: Adventures in Democracy Land.

About the Author

Lemon de Citron is a children's book writer known for her imaginative storytelling and captivating illustrations. Drawing from her unique background and empathetic nature, Lemon crafts stories that teach children about adult subjects like politics, the financial system, and the modern world in a fun and engaging way. Her work aims to inspire young readers to think critically, understand complex topics, and appreciate the world around them.

www.ingramcontent.com/pod-product-compliance
Lightning Source LLC
LaVergne TN
LVHW012115170826
845678LV00014BA/2945

* 9 7 8 1 7 3 8 9 6 4 5 4 3 *